THE
HOME KITCHEN
STARTUP

**360°Guide to start
A Highly Profitable Food Business at home for Low Cost!
Are you ready?**

Ex - Sgt DASGUPTA

Dear Readers,

I am delighted to present to you my book, "The Home Kitchen Startup." This book is the culmination of my personal and professional experiences, and I am excited to share them with you.

As I sit down to write this book, I am overwhelmed with gratitude for the incredible people in my life who have supported and inspired me along the way.

Firstly, I would like to express my deep gratitude to my father. Although he passed away long ago, his impact on my life has been profound. He instilled in me a love of language and a passion for storytelling and I am forever grateful for his guidance and wisdom. As a headmaster and English teacher, he earned immense respect in our town for his dedication to his students. Through this book, I hope to carry on his legacy of sharing knowledge and helping others.

I also want to express my deepest appreciation to my wife, who has been my rock and constant support throughout this entire journey. Her unwavering belief in me and my vision has kept me going through the ups and downs of starting a business from scratch.

And to my son, who has been my biggest cheerleader and source of inspiration. Watching him grow and thrive has given me the drive to create a better future not just for myself, but for my family as a whole. I am proud of him for achieving his dream of serving by flying in the services, I am confident that he will continue to make us proud. My wife and son's love and encouragement have been instrumental in allowing me to pursue my passions and write this book.

As an Air Force veteran, I am thankful for the way the service groomed me well and taught me the importance of discipline, perseverance, and hard work. My transfers allowed me to grow both personally and professionally, and I am grateful for the opportunities I received.

Finally, I want to acknowledge the universe for the abundant blessings and opportunities that have come my way. I am humbled by the experiences that have brought me to this point in my life, where I am able to retire early and enjoy the second half of my life while still young and healthy.

It is with this deep sense of gratitude and purpose that I offer this book to you, dear readers. May it inspire and guide you on your own journey towards creating a life and business that you love and inspire you to take that first step towards financial freedom and living the life you have always dreamed of.

Sincerely,
Ex - Sgt DASGUPTA

CONTENTS

-CHAPTER 1-

Understanding
The Food Industry

we start our food startup journey together, I must

congratulate you on the thought process that you are in right now. Somewhere I know if you are reading this book today, it is either because you want to start your own business or you like cooking, or you are already into a business in the food industry, or the topic of this book intrigues you.

In any case, I will state my reasons why I chose the food industry as my second career. I spent exactly two decades serving in the Indian Air Force. I remember getting up early in the morning to go through the vigorous PT and parades, our Ustad continued giving us a hard time, shouting in our ears, making us run here and there, doing countless pushups, running, climbing ropes jumping here and there around.

No matter what difficulties we had to go through, at the end of those training sessions everything that mattered was nor branded shoes or branded clothes or a luxurious watch or a car or a bike.

In those days, all we waited for was when we hit our mess and fill the stomach with food. It was not just me alone, all my entry mates had the same tendencies. For us breakfast used to be a motivation for the hardships of the day, Lunch used to be a relief to continue what was left in the hardships, and dinner was the last relaxing stop before heading for a peaceful and refreshing sleep. In between, any opportunity to catch up for snacks was the cherry on the cake.

It is said that the army fights with a filled stomach. In those days, I understood the importance of food in our day-to-day lives.

It is when we have luxury of fulfilling our basic needs effortlessly that is when our needs grow. Having served in the forces, I understood one thing very clearly that is even if you are ripped off from all your luxuries, everything that you have with you today and once you have been pulled down to your basic necessities, all your needs shall come down to the basic good old roti kapada aur makaan i.e. Food, clothes and shelter.

Right from the beginning of human civilisation, food has been an important part of our lives. Food is no more a mere need for survival, unlike the Stone Age times wherein humans only existed more or less to fight for food, to kill hunger, and to fill the stomach so that they could go to sleep peacefully.

Needless to say, as we look back today, we have walked way ahead of what food meant for us back then. Today food is not just a basic necessity, it is a way to bring people together, to share love and appreciation, create memories, explore new flavours and ingredients, connect with people on a deeper level, show gratitude, respect and support, express creativity, and bring joy to the lives of the people around us. Food plays a major role in our lives, and its importance can never diminish regardless of the technological advancements we make.

Food is also extremely essential for good emotional health. Enjoying meals together with family and friends can be a great way to strengthen the bond and form beautiful memories. Sharing meals helps form a deep sense of community and can be a powerful way to bond people. Food also provides a feeling of comfort and relief during difficult times causing stress.

Food is also a major representation of culture. Different cultures have their own unique cuisines and traditions that are passed down from generation to generation. Eating a certain food often triggers memories of happy childhood days, family gatherings and special occasions. Food is an inseparable part of important religious ceremonies and celebrations.

For a lot of communities and religions around the world, food is an important source of identity. The kind of food we choose to eat reflects our values, what beliefs we harness in our hearts and our rich heritage. For example, some cultures may prefer certain ingredients or cooking methods, while others may emphasise certain flavours and textures. Food is also a way to express our individuality and creativity.

With the evolution of the symbol of food, human civilisation saw the birth of an important industry called the Food Industry. The food industry is an ever-growing and ever-evolving sector. As the world population continues to increase daily, so the demand for food and its related services too shall increase. From the supply chain to production and the distribution process, there are many opportunities for entrepreneurs, restaurants, governments and other stakeholders all around the globe to capitalise on the growth of the Food Industry.

The food sector is a huge industry and one of the most important parts of the global economy. It has been providing a large number of jobs for decades. The innovation in this sector continues to make this sector an ever-evolving sector. The Food Industries make some major contributions towards economic growth combined with the technologies available in today's world.

From agriculture to food production, it is responsible for providing a large section of the population with the necessary sustenance to survive. With new technologies and practices evolving, this sector is getting bigger and bigger every year, and it is estimated that by 2030, it will reach a massive value of $7 trillion.

The food sector provides an opportunity for new entrepreneurs to start their own businesses in this industry and create something unique for consumers. It can also be used as a platform for more sustainable practices such as organic farming or waste reduction. With its large-scale potential, it's no wonder why the food sector continues to grow in size every year.

The beauty of the food business sector lies in its diversity - from traditional cuisines to fusion dishes, there's something for everyone.

With the right strategy and smart investments, anyone can create a successful business in this sector. From sustainable farming methods to optimising the production processes, there are plenty of ways to make money while making sure that we produce healthy and tasty food.

It is a unique and exciting industry that has captured the imagination of millions of people around the world. From home cooks to celebrity chefs, everyone is drawn to the idea of creating delicious meals and serving them up in style. From delicious cuisines to unique food experiences, the sector has something for everyone. Whether you are looking for a new career or simply want to take your passion into the kitchen, there are countless opportunities in this vibrant and dynamic field.

But what makes this sector so attractive?

Why Food Businesses are a Great Investment?

Food businesses are an attractive option for aspiring entrepreneurs due to their high earning potential while having low capital requirements and a huge potential for growth. From a small pizza shop to a large restaurant chain, there are a variety of food business options available to entrepreneurs.

While all types of businesses have their own unique challenges, food businesses have the potential to be both profitable and enjoyable.

Food businesses are appealing to entrepreneurs because they often require a relatively low amount of capital to get started as compared to the other sectors. The cost of ingredients, equipment, and staffing can be kept low compared to other types of businesses. This means that entrepreneurs can get their businesses up and running quickly and with minimal financial risk. many food businesses don't require a large amount of space, which can help in keeping overhead costs low.

Food businesses have the potential to be very profitable. Many people are willing to pay a premium for quality food, especially if the food is unique or of high quality. The food businesses can benefit from repeat customers who become loyal to their favourite restaurant or food truck. This means that entrepreneurs can build a steady stream of revenue over time, which can help them grow their businesses.

With the right marketing strategies in place, food businesses can expand to multiple locations or even become national or International chains. This can be a great opportunity for entrepreneurs looking to make a large impact in the food industry.

Of course, starting any business comes with a certain amount of risk. Food businesses are no exception. The Food Industry is highly competitive, and entrepreneurs must be prepared to work hard to create a successful business.

Food businesses require a lot of dedication and hard work. However, entrepreneurs can create a successful and profitable food business with the right strategies and developing an eye for detail.

This industry is one of the most attractive business opportunities for small-scale startups. With the rise in demand for convenience and healthy options, there has been an increase in the number of small businesses entering this space.

From meal delivery services to healthy snacks, there is a great potential for small-scale entrepreneurs to enter this market. With the help of digital marketing and affordable technology, entrepreneurs can reach out to their customers more easily and efficiently than ever before.

By developing smart strategies and having a pretty good core team running the startup, a small-scale startup can make an impact in this competitive market. They just need to understand customer needs and find ways to address them better than their competitors. This will ensure their business standing out from the crowd and offers value that customers won't be able to find elsewhere.

This book aims to discuss various aspects of starting an effective small business in the food sector, such as knowing your target market, understanding the laws and regulations related to food manufacturing, learning effective marketing techniques and taking advantage of modern technology.

CHAPTER 2

Why The Food Startups Fail

T

he past year has seen a lot of changes in my locality.

One of the most exciting developments was the opening of a new bakery shop. Three friends, probably in their mid-thirties decided to invest in a shop and set up a bakery.

They invested heavily in the necessary equipment, hired staff, and set up a beautiful display counter. They even had an air conditioning system installed. With everything in place, they had a grand inauguration and the shop was open for business.

At first, the business flourished. The shop was filled with customers, both old and new, who were eager to try out the delicious treats that were on offer. Everyone was thrilled to have a new bakery in the area, and the owners were confident that they had made the right decision.

Unfortunately, the success was short-lived. After a few months, the business began to suffer. The owners had invested a lot of money in the shop and weren't able to cover their costs. They had to make the difficult decision to shut down the business and leave the locality.

The closure of the bakery was a huge blow to the owners as well as to the people employed there.

It was sad to see the bakery close down and the owners had to leave the locality. It was a reminder of the fragility of small businesses and the challenges faced.

Why do so many people fail in their pursuit of creating a successful startup?

The answer lays in the lack of proper preparation. They think that having a great idea and getting funding is enough to make it happen. But what actually needs to happen is a lot more than that in order to turn a dream into a viable business

In the previous few years, there has been a major wave of growth of entrepreneurship in the country, especially after the post-COVID era. The COVID lockdowns suddenly put a halt to the high speed at which the world was running and allowed the world to stop, relax and think.

For a lot of us, those days were some horrible days of our lives, not just from the COVID point of view but also on the financial front wherein we were pushed to the corner of the wall by the financial hardships as well and made us think of some alternative ways to make money because of the massive cut in the pay or getting laid off by the companies.

Those days of hardship revolutionised the economy as well as our daily lives forever. The more you search, the more you will find astonishing and beautiful business stories especially associated with the COVID and the post-COVID era. The stories of success, the stories of great achievement within a very short period of time, the stories of a sudden shift from job to business and it all sounds very exciting.

Probably this is also one of the reasons that you are also planning your own startup. No matter what stage of life you are in, whether you are a student in college or a working professional or a homemaker, looking after the essential needs of the family- in today's time you have the right number of resources easily available around you.

If you are a student, there is no dearth of energy in you, provided you can manage your time well between your studies and your startup with some amount of innovation and little funding. The best part is that you are at the right starting stage with little to nothing at stake while Having access to a large crowd of professors, students from your batch and both junior and senior batches which is a great blessing. you have the opportunity to network, build relationships, and potentially find good clients as well as short list the potential partners to work with. these individuals would form the core team of your business.

For those of you who have a corporate job, this could be the right time for you as well. You may be at the right spot to start a side hustle, thanks to the COVID-19 pandemic and the lockdown. Many companies have started adopting the work-from-home model, and that is exactly why there is a possibility for you to start your very own food business or your food startup As a side hustle without having to sacrifice much on your career front.

As a homemaker, since you're looking to gain financial independence and have the freedom to make your own decisions. you have the right number of resources as well as experiences available to you to start your own food business. Considering you already have been working in your kitchen at home, you know every nook and corner of it like the back of your hand, you have the experience of cooking in your day to day lives, since you understand the needs of the family really well and understand what can really make the difference in the food products you have the ability to put that "maa ke haath ka khaana" magic I.e food cooked by mom magic into your food products . You also have access to other homemakers, with similar needs and expertise, as well as similar resources available that multiplies the productivity and the resources right away while reducing the work load drastically. This is the best form of team one can put in place.

To begin with, this is something that I believe that everyone has done at some point of time in life. It was either a lunch break during your office hours, or visited a random shop to enjoy a cup of tea.

While you were sitting at a tea stall, enjoying the tea, You noticed a lot of crowds around the tea stall and started to wonder how much money this tea seller makes each day; And then immediately jumped to do the maths, trying to calculate the number of a cup of tea he sells in a day thereafter trying to calculate the amount of money he is earning each day multiplying it by the number of days in a month.

At that point of time wondering, probably the numbers were impressive, and you ended up concluding that probably he makes more money than you. At that point of time, it seemed so easy and lucrative. My dear friends in the next section I plan to break the same myth and introduce you to reality.

Reasons why many food startups or the food business fail.

a) During first time the major mistake that a new budding entrepreneur makes is that he forgets to do any study or any kind of market research. Most of the budding entrepreneurs are so high on emotion and are so excited about starting something new. He expects to make a huge profit from day one. And he or she sets off on the path without understanding the integrity of the kind of business he or she is stepping into resulting in making huge losses and bad experiences in the entrepreneurial journey. This is the biggest enemy of any entrepreneur.

b) Having done no research or inadequate research about the product before putting it into the market, as a result, the probability of the success of the product being launched goes down. As a result, the credibility of the business goes down affecting both the sales of the business as well as the morale of the entrepreneur.

c) Too eager to rush to develop a product which they feel might be successful without even giving a thought about their target market. Who will be the end user of the product or services that you plan to launch remains unplanned and as a result, they might end up with an amazing product but the product might not suit the end user.

d) The reason number four why the food startups fail is because the new entrepreneurs are so eager to get their business up and running, they tend to forget to plan their business in the long term. As a result, in the beginning, it does happen that their business is up and running amazingly but as they tend to face a new hurdle, they lack the ability to steer their business across the hurdles because of the lack of their long term thought process.

e) The failure to adapt to changing market trends startups are often faced with the challenge of adapting to the changes in the market trends. Unfortunately, many of these startups fail to do so and end up leading walking through the path of failure. One of the main reasons for this failure is the lack of understanding of the market. If a startup fails to recognise and adjust to the changing market, they are likely to fall behind and eventually fail. No matter how huge your company is, this rule applies to everyone. Companies like kodak and Nokia which dominated the market at one point of time nearly disappeared because of the lack of ability to adapt to the changing market trends. As the market evolves, so should the products and services offered by a food startup.

f) The food-related products are directly related to the health and hygiene of the consumer because of which this industry is subject to some mandatory licenses about which the new entrepreneurs are not aware of. This gets them into the possibility of running the business without having required licenses leading to troubles with the government authorities in future.

g) Another major mistake is a lack of focus on customer engagement. They do not plan about advertising their food and services and are too heavily engrossed towards product development. As a result, the segment of the market in which they have targeted the product fails to reach them resulting in poor sales and poor revenue generation.

h) Trying to do everything alone in business is a mistake that most of the new entrepreneurs make and can prove to be extremely costly. It can lead to burnout, lack of focus, and can be inefficient. It eventually turns this new venture into a disaster

i) The last and the most significant mistake that the new entrepreneur makes is extremely poor financial planning. The business gets up and somehow the sales continue to grow day by day by day but the moment there is a sudden halt and the business faces a major hurdle these businesses run out of money leading to the failure of the business.

While taking the leap from your job to a business is surely a significant one but this switch from a job to business may also turn out to be one of the best decisions of your life.

However, I must tell you that before you take this leap your emphasis must be to understand which direction you need to head to and the right steps you must take to make this decision the best decision of your life.

-CHAPTER 3-

The Mindset

T he process of switching from a job to starting your

very own business is going to be a difficult task, not because of the difficulties that you will face but mainly because you have been used to living from paycheque to paycheque, living all your lives with a sense of financial security and a certain amount of certainty.

There is a major shift in the mindset and attitude that has to be adopted in order how to take this huge leap. The mindset and the attitude of an employee might do not allow you to do well and the field of business. While there is plenty of risks involved in entering the business field, there are plenty of rewards too associated with it.

Even the job that you have been doing is uncertain with respect to a sudden recession leading to another Pay cut or mass layoffs by the company to cut its operating cost. There is a false sense of security just because you need not to really lead the entire organisation and tend to work constantly under some kind of leadership at the organisation.

The herd mentality in jobs also tend to keep individuals in their comfort zone allowing them to continue their life from paycheque to paycheque and working with the motivation of little things like promotions and pay hikes. These promotions and pay hikes are good enough to keep most of the population in the rat race. Even while thinking about starting a business the biggest mistake that an employee makes is that he walks up to his fellow employees and starts asking them for suggestions. Honestly, all their colleagues are living in that same comfort zone and are afraid to come out of that comfort zone and are happy to live on their paycheque.

While the first major hurdle that you need to cross is the major fight that you need to win inside your mind and adjust to the new mindset of an entrepreneur. As an entrepreneur, an individual will have to prepare himself mentally and emotionally and as a result develop that attitude to lead the entire organisation that you are ready to build.

You need to get the absolute belief that you are here to build a huge empire and yes you have the abilities to do it you have the right attitude that is needed, and you are ready for this journey. Say it loud to yourself that yes, I was born for this.

Take out a beautiful diary and sit with a pen. Now ask yourself if you had all the time and all the money that is available in this world, what are all those things that you would like to enjoy in your life? Make a list of the dreams that you want to achieve, write down the kind of lifestyle that you want, instead of making a list of materialistic things genuinely chat down the experiences that you want to enjoy in this life. Make a list of the experiences that you would like to gift to your near and dear ones.

The major issue is while we were young, there were no boundaries to our dreams and our wishes but as we continue to grow older and older and older, we continue to get more and more practical with our goals continued to shrink and we start adjusting to the new reality of the world. While they are still many who continue to dream, I urge you to do the least that is to continue to dream. This dream list will at least allow you not to settle down in the world of mediocrity and will continue to give you strong reasons to keep going towards your goal.

If you want to be an entrepreneur, it's important to get into the mindset of one as soon as possible. It can be a difficult process, but once you do, you will be able to get ideas about your business that you wouldn't have been able to before. Suddenly, you'll start to look at the finer details of how businesses are operating around you, and your mind will become more innovative. The process will start to feel interesting and fun, rather than a burden. Solutions will start to pop up in front of you, and it will give you a morale boost. You'll find yourself full of energy and this energy will flow down to the individuals under your leadership.

Being an entrepreneur isn't easy, but it can be incredibly rewarding. To get the most out of it, you need to put in the work and get into the right mindset. Take the time to look around and observe how other businesses are operating. You never know what you may learn! Learn from your mistakes and don't be afraid to ask for help.

Connect with other entrepreneurs and get advice or support. Networking is key and can help you build valuable relationships. Networking is essential while beginning the journey of entrepreneurship and can help you build valuable relationships. Networking is not only key for entrepreneurs, but for anyone looking to grow in their respective careers. It helps you build relationships with people who can help you reach your goals. You can find networking opportunities in many places, from attending events in your local area to joining online groups.

No matter which type of networking you choose, make sure to be open to meeting new people. You never know who you might meet and what kind of opportunities may arise from those connections. When you attend events, make sure to introduce yourself and exchange contact information with people you meet.

Be sure to follow up after a networking event. Reach out and thank the people you met, and if there was a specific person you had a great conversation with, make sure to stay in touch. You never know when a connection might be helpful to you in the future.

Networking is also a great way to find mentors, who can provide invaluable advice and guidance. Mentors can help you stay motivated and on track when times get tough. They can also provide insight into what it takes to be successful.

Networking can help you find potential customers and partners. You never know who might be interested in what you have to offer, so it's important to put yourself out there. Be sure to take advantage of the opportunities that come your way and use them to your advantage.

In the journey of entrepreneurship make it a habit to take time to reflect your progress. Celebrate the success and use the failures as learning experiences. It's important to stay open to new ideas. Invest in yourself and your business. Find ways to boost your skills and knowledge, whether that's through courses, or by gaining experience through working.
Once you start living with the entrepreneur mindset, these experiences will automatically boost your morale and you will start to find yourself always full of energy. This energy is contagious and somehow finds a way to automatically reach the individuals under your leadership.

 It is extremely important to have a positive attitude and the ability of staying optimistic and enjoying the roller coaster life of the business world while having the ability to celebrate small victories and be able to face the setbacks with little to no regrets.

This roller coaster you have already experienced before. It's just that you were always prepared and be prepared to what was coming ahead in one way or the other even while being unsure of what is likely to happen. As a matter of fact, even while you were completing your schooling, completing your graduation or engineering to that job that you are in present, remember the path was full of uncertainty. There as well you had the ability to work really hard or find a smarter way to get across the hurdles that you faced. You have worked hard for your companies so that to make sure the work is completed on time; you have been able to meet the deadlines earlier. Whatever you learnt in your college little to nothing was applied in the job that you are in present, you had to start again to learn new skills to work for the company.

The journey of entrepreneurship is nothing new, you will be working hard just as before maybe a little more in the beginning but remember this time instead of building your employer's dream and money, you will be building something for yourself. This time again you will have to learn new skills and gather knowledge but remember that you have done this multiple times before as well, in each semester, probably every time you switched your job.

In order to do extremely well in your journey of entrepreneurship you have to understand the difference that lies here, it is that all your life you have had people around you doing the same thing over and over again but out here you will tend to walk alone. Your only support might be your family or the friend with whom you plan to start this business or the better half if you are married. You would have left the herd behind and here you are making your way amongst the elite.

This is no exaggeration. Remember while it is comfortable to live with the herd mentality but here's a fact about 95% of the world's population has access to only 5% of the world's economy, because the 95% of the world's population is living with the herd mentality while only 5% of the rich have access to 95% of the world economy. This 5% of the population at some point of time decided to expand their comfort zone. At the end of the day be it the job or business you will have to face difficulties, but the best part is if you succeed with a business the path is going to be extremely rewarding.

Starting a business is not for the faint-hearted people, you are bound to take risks, a well thought calculated risks which shall benefit your business. You will have to take bold decisions to make it work but as you continue to gain the experience the risk that might seem so big on the first day might not even appear to you as a risk a few years down the line. Those rests appear to be big risks to you in today's date just because of your inexperience in the business world, as your experience continues to grow, the bigger steps you will be able to take but as of now these fights you will have to win inside your mind.

Sometimes things are not as bad or not as difficult as they seem to you. But as you continue to think about the issue again and again, they tend to appear even bigger than they actually are tending to think about situations that might actually not happen. As we move ahead along the book, I will give you simple solutions to these issues to instil the confidence that you require.

The next big shift in your personality that you need to make is to drop your ego. There are a lot of maturities that need to be developed inside you. In the journey of the entrepreneurship, you can no longer act as a boss, you have to develop the qualities that a leader has.

In your job you might have climbed up ladders of seniority whereas today you might be in a position sitting in an office where you expect people to speak to you in an extremely respectful manner. However, as you transition to the business world you will have to stay humble. As the Gujarati say the customer is God, any customer irrespective of his background, financial position, caste creed colour, he will be a part of your business and the source of your business income. If you want to create something great in this life and the business world you will have to drop your ego. As your empire grows, that respect that you expect, and all the recognition will come to you on its own.

Whether you like it or not You will have to be open to learning. Business is an ever-learning process, with the number of uncertainties you are bound to make mistakes but one thing you will have to be prompt about that is learning from the mistakes.

It is also important to inculcate the habit of reading. You cannot have all the experiences nor would you like to always make mistakes and learn every time. Your habit of reading is bound to open your horizon manifolds. It is important to understand and stay updated about what all things are happening and what all new developments are taking place, especially with respect to the food industry is happening not just in the area where you operate but with respect to the country and the world.

Inculcating the reading habit will keep you constantly updated about the latest developments that even you might be able to apply to your existing business easily. The amount of knowledge and understanding you will acquire about your field, your product, and your business will-not only allows you to run the business smoothly but also you will earn the respect of the individuals under your leadership.

The switch from your job to the path of building a business will be full of challenges, The path will be full of uncertainty, but those challenges and the difficulties that you are going to face are not going to be as big as it seems to be. With the right mindset and proper preparation, all this that you aim to achieve can be done successfully. It's important to remember to stay focused, remain flexible and stay highly motivated throughout the process good luck!

-CHAPTER 4-

The Vision

N

ow comes the next building block of your

startup, which is defining a vision.

Defining a vision is a crucial step in any startup. It is important to have a clear vision of what the company is aiming to achieve. This vision should be the guiding force behind all decisions made by the company. It should be something that everyone involved in the startup can agree on and work towards.

It is also important to consider the strengths and weaknesses of the company. This can help to identify areas that need improvement and potential opportunities to capitalise on.

It's important to understand that running a successful food business requires careful planning and preparation. Before diving into the food business, it's important to create a vision that will help you develop a strategy and stay on track.

To be successful, you need to have a clear understanding of your goals and objectives. Your vision should be a concise and clear statement that outlines what you want to accomplish. Ensure that you have a clear roadmap and this vision you are about to define now will be the foundation upon which you build your business.

Your vision should be realistic yet ambitious. It will be the driving force behind its growth and development. A vision should be able to be adapted and evolved to meet the changing needs of the company.

Having a realistic vision is essential to the success of a company.

The vision should be something that is achievable within a certain period of time and that the resources available are sufficient to reach them. It should also be something that the company can commit to and work towards.

A vision should be based on sound research and should take into account the present market conditions and trends.

At the same time, a vision should be ambitious. It should set challenging goals that push your very own company to strive for excellence. It should be aspirational and set a high bar for success. This can inspire employees and get them excited about the company's future, and can also attract investors and customers as the company starts to show a promising future.

When defining a vision, it is important to take the time to think about the big picture and think from the long-term perspective of the company which means that the vision should be flexible and should be able to adapt to the changing market conditions and customer needs. It should be able to evolve as the company grows and develops.

As your business grows and changes, you may need to adjust your vision to reflect these changes. This will help ensure that your business remains on track and successful.

Also, consider the company's culture when creating a vision. The vision should reflect the values and beliefs of the company and should be something that once your company grows into a huge business and you have employees working for the company that you have built, those values can get the employees strive for. It should be something that motivates and inspires them.

A vision should be achievable. It should be realistic and should be something that can be achieved with the resources available. It should be something that the company can work towards and strive to achieve. This can include things such as

What is the purpose of the company?

What are your goals for the business in the short term?

Where do you look at the company in long term?

How will it make money?

How will it serve its customers?

How will it stand out from the competition?

What type of food do you want to offer?

What kind of atmosphere do you want to create?

Answering these questions will help you determine the direction of your business and create a plan that will help you achieve success. This will ensure that you stay focused and on track to achieving your business goals in the longer run.

The vision must be easy to understand, it's the blueprint that outlines the goals and objectives of the business, as well as the strategies and tactics you have in mind to achieve them. However, many entrepreneurs tend to make their plans overly complicated, which can lead to confusion and make it difficult to get the business off the ground. Keeping the food business plan simple can ensure success.

-CHAPTER 5-

The Research

T here are just a few of the steps to consider when preparing a plan for a food business. It's important to remember that creating a successful food business is a long-term process and requires careful planning and preparation. Creating a plan for your business will help you stay organised as well as, stay on track, and reach your goals.

While you plan to start a scalable business the first and foremost thing to keep in mind is to identify a unique food product that can be sold. This can be anything from a unique recipe that is not available elsewhere, to a new type of food that is not yet on the market.

To identify this unique product a mixture of your passion for cooking, a lot of experimentation and a lot of market research will be the key. It is important to create a product that is unique enough that it will draw the attention of the customers and draw them towards your product.

Let's focus on how to identify the product that you are going to sell. First and most important of all is to identify what is your comfort zone. Is it baking and producing bakery products, do you want to start with providing your customers with daily meals, Or do you have that unique secret pickle recipe which you feel is likely to be a big hit?

Once you have made a note of the sub-sector where you feel you are comfortable operating, now start with the market research.

Research is cheap but a good amount of research will definitely give you the best of the rewards. It is an important component of any business venture and especially important for food businesses. Instead of trying to rush through things, take time to do a detailed research study about each and every aspect related to your business.

Research allows entrepreneurs to gain insight into the market. As an entrepreneur, you need to be constantly aware of the market you are operating in. You need to know what products and services are selling well, what trends are emerging, and what potential customers are looking for.

But as the market evolves and changes, it can be hard to keep up. That's why it's important to rely on data to gain insight into the market. Data can provide you with valuable information about your target market, what products and services they are interested in, how much they are willing to pay, and more.

By leveraging data, you can make informed decisions about their businesses and ensure they are taking advantage of the right opportunities.

Data can also help you to understand your competitors and how they are operating. By tracking your competitors' prices, marketing strategies, and customer service, you can gain insight into what is working and what isn't.

This can help you to determine how you can differentiate your own business and create a competitive advantage. This strategy can also be used to identify potential customers and their needs. This research can help you to identify potential opportunities and develop strategies to capitalise on them.

By analysing customer data, you can determine who your potential customers are, what they are looking for, and how to reach them. This information can be used to create targeted marketing campaigns and tailor products and services to meet those needs. This will make sure that the products, services, and strategies are well-suited to the market and will be successful.

Data can also help you to understand the food industry well and the trends that are happening within it. By tracking industry data, you can ensure to stay ahead of the curve and be prepared for any changes in the market. This can help you anticipate customer needs and stay competitive.

The first step in any research process is to understand the market. This involves researching the industry, the competition, and the customer base. You should identify the size and scope of the food industry, analyse the existing competition, and understand the customer's needs and preferences.

It's important to read about successful food businesses and understand what it takes to make them successful. Doing your research can help you understand the ins and outs of the food industry, as well as the challenges and opportunities you may face. It's important to look at the successes and failures of past food businesses to see what strategies worked and what didn't.

One of the best ways to learn about successful food businesses is to read case studies and interviews with their owners. These stories provide valuable insight into the strategies and tactics that made the business successful. Reading these stories can provide you with ideas and inspiration for your own food business.

Read about food trends and customer preferences. What is popular in the food industry today? What new products or services are people looking for? Staying on top of food trends can help you stay ahead of the competition and offer customers something new and exciting.

Reading the reviews of food businesses helps to understand customers likes and dislikes. This can help you understand what works and what needs to be improved. Listening to customer feedback is a great way to improve your business and ensure customer satisfaction.

The most important step in launching a successful food product is to identify a need in the marketplace. This requires a thorough understanding of the industry and an ability to identify emerging trends and consumer desires. To determine your target market is to define the characteristics of your product. Is it a healthy snack? A meal replacement? An indulgent treat? Once you have identified the characteristics of your food product, you can start to narrow down your target market.

For example, if you are launching a healthy snack, your target market will likely be health-conscious individuals who are looking for a nutritious snack. On the other hand, if you are launching an indulgent treat, your target market will likely be people who are looking for a sweet, rich snack.

Once you have identified the characteristics of your product and the type of consumer it appeals to, you can start to look at demographics.
Who are the most likely people to purchase your product?

Are they college students or working professionals?

Are they men or women?

Are they from a certain age group?

Answering these questions will certainly give you meaningful answers to the research you have been conducting. Understand that There is a high probability that there is a existing similar product available in the market however There is a specific need that Your customers are looking for which is not available at present in the market. This is known as the void in the market.

You must take the time to identify areas where their product can fill a void. Answering these questions will certainly give you meaningful answers to the research you have been conducting. Understand that There is a high probability that there is a existing similar product available in the market however There is a specific need that Your customers are looking for which is not available at present in the market. This is known as the void in the market.

You must take the time and patience to identify the areas where your product can fill a void. Gathering customer feedback is an extremely effective way to identify the void in the market. start looking for some kind of patterns in the feedback from your potential customers. If many people are saying that they need a particular feature then it is likely that there is a void in the market for a product or service that provides that feature. Similarly, if a lot of customers are dissatisfied with the customer service that they are receiving from the existing providers, then you could look to provide better customer service as a part of your product or service.

When conducting the customer feedback, make sure to ask open-ended questions which will allow the potential customers to express their thoughts and feelings. Questions could include:

"What do you like most about existing products or services in the market?"

"What do you think is missing from existing products or services in the market?"

"What would you like to see more of in the market in the future?"

By asking these types of questions, your potential customers can be given the opportunity to express their opinions and their needs freely, which can in turn help you to identify any voids in the market. If you can thoroughly understand this void in the existing market congratulations You are now looking at the perfect opportunity to fill this gap And provide that missing value to your customers as well as capitalise on this opportunity.

Instead of just focusing on selling the product and making money, think what value can you provide to your customers, The more you focus about the benefits of your customer the more the customer will bring benefit to you which and turn will create a healthy growth in your business. The value and money go hand in hand.

Your homework has to be solid. How solid your business is going to be will depend on how Diligently you have done your homework.

CHAPTER 6

The Benefits of Starting Small and Scaling Big

Starting this home food business is definitely not going to be an easy task and it's natural to aspire to aim for the big right from the start. it's tempting to go all-in, investing in the latest kitchen equipment and advertising your services in the local paper. But, if you don't have the experience or the resources to back it up, this can be a recipe for disaster.

The story of the three friends and their bakery from chapter 2 is a reminder of the importance of careful planning and decision-making when it comes to business investments. Investing in a business is a high-risk endeavour and it is essential to make sure that the initial costs are covered and that there is enough cash flow to sustain the business in the long term.

It is also important to be realistic about the potential returns on any investment however even after developing a robust entrepreneurial mindset, nurturing a big and healthy vision and putting together solid research in place yet there are unforeseen circumstances and situations which you might not have catered for. It is impossible to do so until you have some experience with you. Most of the individuals starting a business especially those who do not have a business background are likely to run into tough spots and even dead ends and it's okay to happen.

The attitude of staying positive, willing to learn as well as staying cash rich in those times is something that will surely make you successful in long run. However, if all your savings and capital is invested right away, it's natural that instead of learning, your fear will take over and not let you think and learn clearly, you will be forced to take steps that you might not take if you had enough reserve money to start again.

Round one of your entrepreneurial journeys is generally to learn and experience. If you pick most of the successful businessmen today, 80-90% of them had one or two failed attempts before they found the perfect recipe that works for them. It happened with me as well and might happen with you, it's smarter to embrace this fact but I can assure you that you will eventually discover that recipe that will eventually pull you out of the rat race and allow you to live the lives of your dream.

Therefore, starting small and taking things one step at a time is a smart way to make sure your business succeeds in the long run.

What are the Benefits of Starting Small?

Starting with a small investment will have several benefits, which includes:

This will allow you to start with a Lower financial risk: By starting small, you can minimise the financial risk and ensure that you're not putting your personal finances at stake. This also gives you the room to make mistakes and in case of a financial loss you have enough funds available to again start afresh. This time with some very important experiences which will come handy in your round two.

Building a customer base: By starting small, you can focus on building a loyal customer base and providing excellent customer service while it is easier for you to manage the administration related issues pretty easily.

Testing your business model: Starting small will allow you to test your business model and refine your offerings before investing a significant amount of time and money while allowing you to, understand the issues related to the business model and resolve it easily.

Flexibility: Starting small gives you the flexibility to make changes It even allows you to entirely switch to a new business model if you realise the previous one is not working out, this can be achieved relatively easily without hurting your finances much and pivot your business model whenever needed.

How to Start Small?

No matter whether Starting with a small investment or a large investment, the basic fundamental is a careful planning and strategy. Here are some tips for getting started:

Focus on one or two core produces: this point has been discussed amply earlier. How ever in context to the topic in discussion here, it makes your administration easier and makes the overall business model much cheaper to start with without compromising the quality of the product.

Use your existing resources: Starting small will further allow you to start with much smaller investment since you will be able to use your existing equipment and resources available at home to get started. For example, you can use your home kitchen and appliances to prepare your products.

Keep your costs low: keep a Look out for ways and means to keep your costs low, such as sourcing affordable ingredients and packaging, how ever do not compromise on the quality and the rich look of the packaging

Focus on customer service: By providing excellent customer service, you can build a loyal customer base that will help you grow your business over time. In any case, keep a good communication with this costumer base to make sure they stick to your products for their needs.

What is the Strategy for Scaling Up?

Once you've successfully established your business , you have a proven business model that works for the kind of product and business you plan to set up. You have successfully build a good sized costumer base and the orders continue to grow day by day. Your business has generated some revenue and it's difficult to run your business with the existing equipment's, it's time to start thinking about scaling up.

Some strategies for growing your business over time are:

Reinvest your profits: Instead of taking all of your profits out of the business, reinvest some of them back into the business to fuel growth.

Expand your product line: Once you have established your core offering, consider expanding your product line to cater to a wider audience. Towards this you will be required to invest into a good equipment's and set up a good commercial kitchen.

Build a team: it's would be foolish to try and run everything on your own, this approach will clip your growth and also make it difficult for you to run this business.

Build partnerships: Look for opportunities to partner with other businesses or organisations to reach new customers and expand your reach.

Invest in marketing: As your business grows, it's essential to invest well into in marketing to reach a wider audience and increase your visibility.

Though this chapter is just an outline of how to go about all your processes, the major aim was to stop you from jumping into this venture with all you have and allow you to have a room to experiment as well as experience without having to invest a large amount. The following chapters will walk you through the detailed process of each step involved into building a big successful food business.

CHAPTER 7

The Power of a Team: How to Build an Effective Startup Team from Scratch

As a business owner, it can be tempting to try and do everything yourself. After all, you're the one with the vision, right? You know your business better than anyone else, so why not just do it all on your own?

Unfortunately, trying to do everything yourself can be a major mistake. Not only can it be a huge drain on your time and energy, but it can also be a huge waste of money. By taking on too many tasks, you're not only robbing yourself of valuable time, but you're also missing out on the expertise of others.

When launching a food startup, many entrepreneurs are focused solely on the product they are creating and do not realise the importance of having a team. Although it may seem like running a startup alone is the best way to save money and resources, it can actually cost the business more in the long run.

One example of this can be seen in the story of an entrepreneur who also happened to be a good friend of mine in Vadodara who started a meal delivery business as well as he had a counter where he served the costumers walking up to his shop. He was passionate about his product and believed that he knew his business better than anyone else. He wanted to be in charge of every aspect of the startup, from cooking and packaging to delivery.

At first, he was able to handle everything on his own. He was able to cook the food, package it, and deliver it to customers. He was proud of his ability to multitask and believed that he was saving the business money by doing everything himself.

However, as the business grew, he found that he was struggling to keep up with demand. He was working long hours and becoming exhausted, which affected the quality of his food and the delivery times.

Despite the initial success of his startup, he realised that he needed help if he wanted to take his business to the next level. He decided to put together a small team to help him with the cooking, packaging, and delivery.

While it was initially difficult for him to work in a team setup, he soon realised that having a team allowed him to focus on the bigger picture. He was able to spend more time developing new menu items, improving the customer experience, and expanding the business.

The business continued to grow and thrive, but he recognised that his initial mistake of trying to do everything himself had cost him valuable time and resources. He realised that by hiring a team, he was able to save money in the long run and achieve greater success than he ever could have on his own.

Having a team of dedicated team to help manage the business can help a startup grow and succeed. This story serves as an example of how important it is for entrepreneurs to understand their limitations and be willing to ask for help. Many entrepreneurs are passionate and driven, but they often overestimate their abilities and try to tackle too much on their own.

What are the benefits of having a team with you?

The first benefit of having a team is that it can help to divide and conquer tasks. As the business grows and more is expected from the entrepreneur, having a team to help manage different aspects of the business can be invaluable. Having a team to help with marketing, research, product development, and customer service can free up the entrepreneur to focus on the bigger picture.

Another benefit of having a team is that it can help to bring in new ideas and perspectives. Having a diverse group can bring a variety of ideas to the table that can help the business grow. A team that is open to change and willing to think outside the box can help move the business forward.

As an entrepreneur, you have a vision for your startup that goes beyond just creating a product. You want to create an entire organisation and build a team that will help you achieve your vision.

But how do you go about doing this?

Creating an entire business from your home is no small feat. It requires a great deal of planning and foresight, and it takes a team of dedicated people to make it happen. it's not enough to just have a great product. We need to think bigger if we want to succeed.

Team building is an essential part of any successful business. A strong team can help an organisation reach its goals and objectives more quickly and efficiently. As a leader of a team, it is important to understand the importance of team building and to take the necessary steps to create a strong team. That's why factoring in a team is essential to help us get off the ground.

In order to achieve the the task of building the team successfully the following strategies are recommended.

Step 1: Pick the Right Individuals for Your Team

The first step in creating a startup from your home is to build the right team. A team of highly motivated and talented individuals is essential for success. It's important to assemble a team no matter if it comprises of your close friend or a few friends or your close family members, or a combination of both however, it's important when you are all set to look for the core team of the co- founders to set up your business, it's important to be with the people you trust the most, and it is equally important to start the journey with the individuals with whom your mindset and the frequency matches.

When looking for your team, look for people who are passionate about the mission of the organisation that you all are ready to build.

All the members of this team must also be open to meeting new challenges and taking over of roles and responsibilities and be willing to work hard to achieve goals. Having the right team on board is key to achieving success.

Step 2: Develop an Effective Organisational Structure

The second step in building a startup from home is to develop an effective organisational structure for the team. This should include the roles and responsibilities of each team member. This will help to ensure that each team member knows exactly what their role is and what they need to do in order to help the business succeed.

It's also important to consider the decision-making process. This should be clearly laid out and agreed upon by all team members so that everyone knows who is responsible for making decisions and how those decisions should be made. This will help to ensure that everyone is on the same page and that the business is able to move forward positively and productively.

Once the roles and responsibilities of each team member and the decision-making process have been established, it's important to ensure a clear chain of command.

This means that there is a clear understanding of who is responsible for what and who should be consulted in order to make decisions.

It's important to ensure that the organisational structure is flexible and can adapt to the needs of the business. As the business grows, the organisational structure will likely need to change in order to meet the needs of the business. It's important to ensure that the structure is able to adapt to these changes and that the roles and responsibilities of each team member are able to be adjusted accordingly.

It's important to create an organisational structure that is both efficient and effective. This will ensure that the team is able to operate optimally.

Step 3: Establish Effective Communication

The third step in creating a startup from home is to establish effective communication. This includes both internal and external communication.

Internal communication is the way that you communicate with your team and partners. Any startup needs to ensure that everyone involved is on the same page and working towards the same goal and everyone knows what is expected of them. This requires clear communication, both verbal and written, as well as an open and transparent environment.

The next step is to establish a process for feedback. This process should include a way for team members to provide feedback on the developments and products itself. This feedback can then be used to make improvements and ensure that the process is effective.

Step 5: Create a Culture of Learning

The fifth step in creating a startup from home is to create a culture of learning. This means that everyone on the team should be open to learning new skills and knowledge about new fields.

It helps to foster an environment of collaboration and creativity and allows the team members to develop their skills. It also encourages employees to take the initiative and come up with new ideas and solutions, which can help drive the business's success.

So, what are the steps to creating a learning culture within your startup?

Set up a learning environment. This means having a space that is conducive to learning. It should be well organised and well-equipped. This could be a physical space, such as an office, or it could be an online space, such as a virtual classroom, based on the size of the house available.

Provide the necessary resources for learning. This could include books, videos, and other materials that can be used to gain knowledge about topics relevant to your business. It's also important to provide access to online courses, such as those offered by Udemy, Coursera, etc. These can help to ensure that the team is up-to-date with the latest trends and technologies.

Take out some time off the huddle to create an opportunity for the start-up team to share their knowledge with each other. This could be done through regular meetings, webinars, or even online forums. This will help to create a sense of community within the startup, enabling everyone to learn from each other and share ideas.

Try to ensure that the learning culture is sustained. This could be done through regular check-ins, feedback sessions, or even mentorship programs. This will help to ensure that the team is motivated to continue to learn and grow.

Creating a learning culture will help ensure that the organisation can adapt and evolve as needed. This will help the organisation stay competitive in an ever-changing marketplace.

Step 6: Foster Collaboration

The sixth step in creating a successful startup from home is to foster collaboration. Collaboration is essential for success, as it allows for different perspectives and ideas to be shared.

It's important to create an environment where everyone feels comfortable sharing their thoughts and opinions. This will ensure that the team is able to make the best decisions and achieve its goals.

Step 7: Build a strong bond amongst the team

A successful team must have a strong sense of unity and purpose. Team members must trust and respect each other and feel that they are part of something bigger. It is your responsibility to ensure that team members feel a personal connection to the team.

It is important to ensure that the team members are well-acquainted with each other. This can be done by organising team-building activities that foster a sense of camaraderie and collaboration. These activities can be anything from group meals and group outings to team sports or creative projects.

You as well as all your team members must invest the time to get to know each team member and their families, and to be aware of any issues they may be facing personally or professionally. Showing empathy and providing support whenever possible will help to build loyalty and trust among team members.

Another way of creating that strong bond is largely based on how you deal with disputes. As a leader, it's important to be fair and impartial when dealing with any disputes or issues that arise. It's essential to be consistent in your approach and to ensure that all team members are given a fair and equal opportunity to voice their opinions and be heard.

Creating a sense of belonging and loyalty among team members is something that will hold your team together over long term. It is up to you as the leader to cultivate an environment of trust and respect, and to provide team members with opportunities to make meaningful contributions to their team's success.

The team building is not a one-off event. It's an ongoing process and it's important to stay connected and engaged with the team.

The steps mentioned above would help you to build a strong team, provided you constantly make efforts to keep a strong unified team and your active involvement is seen and felt with the team.

However, despite having discussed all the steps on how to build a strong team, it can still be a confusing and overwhelming process. Even with the best of intentions, you may find yourself feeling lost and unsure of what to do next.

This is perfectly normal and understandable, the process of creating a successful team is often full of trial and error. In fact everything about the business is full of trial and error. Every situation and every challenge you might face can never be put into black and white, hence it's smart to study about other successful businesses, it can provide valuable insights and ideas for building a strong team. By researching other companies in your industry or related fields, you can learn about their strategies for hiring, training, and retaining top talent.

You can also study the culture and values of successful businesses. Look for the following answers: -

How do they encourage a positive and productive work environment?

What kind of leadership do they promote?

What are their communication and collaboration practices?

By examining these factors, you can gain a better understanding of what it takes to create a high-performing team. You can use this knowledge to identify areas where your team can improve and develop new strategies to enhance team dynamics.

Another way to learn from other businesses is to network with other entrepreneurs and business leaders. Attend industry events, join professional organisations, and participate in online communities to connect with others in your field. By sharing ideas and experiences with others, you can gain new perspectives on team building and find solutions to common challenges.

In conclusion, building a strong team is an inseparable component of any successful startup. No matter how talented or capable you may be as a founder, you cannot build a successful business alone. It takes a team of trusted, hardworking individuals who are committed to the startup's vision and mission to achieve success.

However, building a strong team is not a one-time effort but an ongoing process that requires continuous learning, improvement, and investment. With time as your team will face one challenge after another and overcome all of those challenges while watching out for each other, the teams bonding will get even stronger, leading to greater loyalty and accountability for the startup's success.

All your team members are a strong pillar of the business, but the strongest pillar is you, are you an effective leader? It's time to invest some good amount of time in your leadership qualities.

-CHAPTER 8-

The Strongest Pillar of the Team Is You!

T he previous chapter clearly outlined how important the process of team building is for your organisation to reach its goals and objectives more quickly and efficiently as well as the steps you need to ensure as a leader or founder of this startup to build this efficient team.

It must have been amply clear by now that this task is going to be demanding but one thing I can assure you, that is the rewards are going to be far greater, and once you will look back at these instances in the future, you will definitely cherish it, hopefully while comfortably enjoying the early retirement.

In order to achieve the task of building the team and lead them through the vision of your startup successfully, you must work on yourself and develop the qualities of a leader. In the military we call it the officer like qualities. The military style of leadership is one of the best types of leaderships seen around the world and has proved to be effective even during the worst times in the history of human kind which has made history.

Personally, during my service tenure I have seen the kind of miracles, this type of leadership can do. Even at the most inhospitable places of the country, away from the civilisations, every member of the team had to struggle for the basic necessities yet it was the feeling of camaraderie, the sense of being a part of the unit and the level of trust in each other, each member of the team would look out for each other as well as each and every member knew exactly what was his role and put in the best of their efforts to deliver what is expected out of them.

What is the military style of leadership?

The military style of leadership is one that is based on an organised structure and gives importance to a strict adherence to rules and regulations.

The leader sets the tone for the organisation, and sets the standards for behaviour and performance for everyone in the organisation. This does not mean he enforces everything on everyone while the leader can do as he wishes. The leader is expected to be a role model, and set the example for the rest of the team.

The leader is also expected to provide clear direction, and communicate the mission and objectives of the organisation. Leaders in the military style of leadership are expected to be decisive in their decisions, and take responsibility for those decisions.

They are expected to provide constructive feedback and guidance to the team, and be able to take charge when needed. The leader must also be able to delegate tasks and provide support to the team.

The military style of leadership also has a focus on discipline and order. The leader is expected to look after the rules and regulations of the organisation, and ensure that everyone is following them.

The leader must also be able to motivate and inspire the team to work together and achieve the goals of the organisation. The leader is also expected to be fair and consistent in their decisions and actions.

This style of leadership also emphasises the importance of team work. The leader is expected to be able to build strong relationships with the team, and foster an environment of camaraderie and trust.

The leader should also be able to recognise the strengths and weaknesses of the team, and be able to utilise them to achieve the desired outcomes.

The leader must also be able to manage conflicts and difficult situations in a professional manner. They should be able to maintain good communication with the team, and be able to provide clear guidance and direction when needed.

In this style of leadership, the leader should be able to recognise the importance of training and development, and provide the resources necessary to ensure that the team is prepared and equipped to meet the challenges they may face.

The military style of leadership is also one of the best style of leadership because it stays away from any kind of politics, hence each and everyone focuses solely on the task. The mission stays paramount. It can be a powerful tool for driving performance and achieving success. It is important to understand that this type of leadership requires a great deal of commitment and dedication from the leader, as a result it is not suitable for everyone.

However, since you are the founder of your organisation, your capital is at stake, your dreams and your future depend on the success of your startup, the required level of commitment and dedication is a must and as a result this style of leadership might be a right fit for you.

What exact leadership qualities do you need to inculcate?

The following qualities are referred as the 15 officers like qualities in the military. These qualities are divided among four factors they are

1. Planning and Organising

    Effective Intelligence
    Reasoning Ability

Power Of Expression
Organising Ability

2. Social Adjustment
   Social Adaptability
   Sense of Responsibility
   Co-operation
    Self Confidence

3. Social Effectiveness

Initiative
   Ability to Influence the Group
   Speed of making Decision
Liveliness

4. Dynamic

   Determination
   Courage
   Stamina

As a founder of a startup, it is essential to hone your leadership skills and develop as an influential leader. To achieve this, you must focus on developing these key qualities, we'll take a closer look at each of these qualities and how you can develop them as a leader.

<u>Factor one: Planning and Organising</u>

Planning and organising are the key skills to start with that will help you to effectively manage your resources, your team and your business. This falls under first of the four key factors which includes having an effective intelligence, reasoning ability, power of expression and organising ability. In simple words it means how jugaadu are you? Let's take a closer look at each of these qualities

Effective intelligence: - This is a must-have quality for you. It is the ability to think quickly and accurately and to be able to solve problems.

It is essential to be able to make decisions with confidence, this will help you to handle any unforeseen situations that you might have to face on day-to-day basis. It is also important to be able to think strategically and to be able to anticipate future trends to be able to run the business smoothly.

To be able to develop this quality the first thing you need to learn is to look at things practically not emotionally. Focus on getting more and more exposures so as to ensure that you get to face new situations and face them, think of solutions, it's okay to make mistakes along the process, important is to grow as a individual, grow as a leader.

Reasoning ability: - This is the ability to think logically, to analyse data and to make sound decisions. This skill will allow you in making practical decisions to be able to evaluate a situation and to be able to come to a conclusion that is based on facts and evidence.

To be able to develop this quality you must read and increase your knowledge base, start taking decisions about every small and big thing in your life and more importantly know the whys of every decisions you take.

Keep the the purpose in mind for every decision you take, You must be able to answer why you have said or done something in a particular way. You cannot be someone who takes random decisions or says anything without thinking first.

Power of expression:- This is the ability to communicate effectively and to be able to express your ideas clearly. It is important to be able to present your ideas in a way that clear and crisp as well as understandable by all.

As the founder of the startup, you will be involved into a lot of planning and discussions with your team. As a result, you must be able to Convey your ideas and plans accurately to your team, this forms a important part of the leadership personality that you possess.

In order to develop a good power of expression, it's important to be a good listener first, once you understand what the next person wants to say and more importantly what he wants to communicate and why, and then respond then your response automatically improves right away.

Another way to develop your power of expression is by Participate in conversations, talk to other people especially the ones you feel are good at expressing and indulge into heathy discussions with them.

Organising ability:- It is the ability to manage resources, to plan and delegate tasks. It is important to be able to prioritise tasks and to be able to make sure that tasks are completed on time.

To improve the quality, you must start to by practicing the following small things in your day to day lives

      a)   Plan and organise your time

      b)   Lookout for the next day and plan how you can make best use of it

      c)   Presently in your job or wherever you are, whenever a work is handed over to you, don't just start to work, take some time to plan and organise how you are going to do this work efficiently and in minimum time

These qualities are essential for a leader and are essential for the success of a startup. Being passionate about work is one thing, to be able to properly stay organised and developing yourself as a skilled planner and accomplished strategist is another game all together.

Factor two: Social adjustment

The factor two focuses on another important aspect of leadership that is the ability to quickly adjust to changing social environments, adjust amongst new people you have just met. This is the base to develop your qualities to be able to lead and develop your team.

It's difficult to imagine a leader leading a team while finding a hard time to gel with the team members. Hence, to be able to lead your team, you must work towards developing your abilities to work in your team comfortably while keeping it together. This factor focuses on your social aspects while working in a group. let's take a closer look at these qualities

Social Adjustment:- It is the ability to adjust to new situations, environments, and people. It's an important quality for any leader to have, as it allows you to quickly and easily adapt to the changing needs of your team, adjust to having new people around you as well as adjust to the changing needs of your business.

This means focusing on developing a range of qualities which includes social adaptability, a sense of responsibility, co-operation, and self-confidence.

To develop this quality as a leader, you should take the time to get to know your team and understand their individual strengths and weaknesses. This will help you to create an environment that encourages collaboration and open communication.

Social adaptability:- It is the ability to understand and relate to different people, cultures, and situations. As a leader, it's important to be able to recognise the unique needs and perspectives of each team member. This will help you to create an environment where everyone feels valued and respected.

To develop this quality, you should take the time to get to know your team members and understand their individual backgrounds and experiences. You should also be open to new ideas and perspectives, and be willing to listen and learn from your team.

A sense of responsibility:- This is the back bone of all the leadership qualities. As the founder of a startup, you need to be able to take responsibility for the successes and failures of your team.

To develop this quality, you should strive to be consistent and reliable, and be willing to take ownership of the decisions made by the team.

The more important aspect of this quality is to imbibe the quality of having the courage to accept mistakes, talking ownership of the team's mistakes and thereafter proceeding to correct that mistake.

This very quality will set you apart from the crowd and establish you as a good leadership of the team. This will help to create an atmosphere of trust and accountability within your team.

Co-operation:- This quality is paramount not just for you as a leader but for every team member for the team to operate with the best Co-ordination possible to make the startup successful.

As a leader, it's important to be able to foster a sense of collaboration and camaraderie. To develop this quality, you should encourage open communication between team members and create an environment where everyone feels comfortable voicing their opinions and ideas.

You should also be willing to lend a helping hand when needed, and be open to feedback and constructive criticism.

Self-confidence:- It is a key quality for you to be able to utilise all the qualities and take decisions without questioning your abilities. In very Simple words self confidence is having trust in your own self and have trust in you own abilities, qualities and judgement.

Let me help you with another perspective to understand how important this quality is,

Have you ever seen any leader Who is doubtful or confused in general?

No right? Exactly, it's an inseparable part of a leader. Confidence plays a great role in developing your personality & Overall growth. Hence, it's important to have faith in your own abilities and decisions, and be able to make decisions confidently and quickly. This will not happen overnight.

To develop this quality, you should take the time to understand your strengths and weaknesses, read a lot to improve your knowledge and strive to improve in areas where you are lacking.

You should also take the time to celebrate your successes, and remember that mistakes are an important part of the learning process.

Social adjustment is a critical skill for you as the startup founder, you will need these qualities to navigate new situations, conflicts and build important relationships. Ultimately, the ability to adjust to new situations and people is key for you as well as for the team members looking to build a strong network, and navigate the challenges of entrepreneurship.

Factor three: Social Effectiveness

The factor three focuses on another important aspect of leadership that is the ability to be able to set the tone for the direction of the company and be able to effectively communicate your vision and values to your team, to be able to lead and develop your team, once your qualities of social adjustments are strong. To do this, you must focus on developing certain qualities as a leader. Let's take a closer look at each of these qualities.

Social Effectiveness:- It is the ability which ensures that you're able to effectively communicate with your team and build relationships. This means being able to listen to other people's opinions, giving constructive criticism, and having a good understanding of how to motivate and inspire your team.

You must be able to build trust and respect among your team members so that everyone feels comfortable sharing their ideas. These include developing qualities like initiative, ability to influence the group, speed of making decisions, and liveliness.

Initiative:- Initiative is a quality that is highly valued in many contexts. It is the ability to take charge of a situation and act without waiting for any instruction or direction. People with initiative are proactive and self-motivated, and are willing to take risks and be creative.

These individuals identify problems or opportunities and take the necessary steps to address them without external prompting. This quality demonstrates a person's willingness to take ownership of their actions and can be beneficial in both the workplace and in personal life.

Aa leader, you must be able to take the initiative and make decisions that will benefit the company. This includes anticipating potential problems, coming up with creative solutions, and having the courage to make difficult decisions. You must also be able to think on your feet and take action quickly when necessary.

Ability to influence a group:- As a leader, it is important to be able to effectively influence a group in order to achieve success. This involves developing an understanding of the team's needs and motivations, and being able to communicate with them in a way that resonates.

You should also be able to adapt their approach to different personalities and communication styles, and build relationships with the team members that are based on trust and respect.

Leaders who possess the ability to influence a group can have a profound impact on their team's performance. They are able to bring out the best in each individual and foster a culture of collaboration and trust. This quality is particularly valuable in today's fast-paced and ever-changing business environment, as it enables leaders to quickly respond to changing circumstances and leverage their team's collective skills and knowledge to drive results.

In order to move the company forward, you should be able to inspire the team to work together towards a common goal, and motivate them to take the necessary actions to achieve the goals. This means being able to effectively manage conflict, inspire others, and create a sense of unity and purpose.

Speed of Decisions:- This quality is self understood, As a leader, it's important that you're able to make decisions quickly and effectively. This means being able to weigh the pros and cons of a situation and come to a conclusion quickly.

In the entrepreneurial journey, you will be tossed around by various situations developing on almost every second day, your resources and options will be limited, in that situation the outcome of the situation will depend on how quickly and effectively you can take a sound decision and act on it.

How good are you at handling situations quickly and act on it is directly interlinked with a number of qualities mentioned before.
First in the list would be effective intelligence, the stronger you develop this quality, the easy it becomes to quickly look at a situation, analyse it and think of a solution.

Self confidence plays another key role in allowing you to take quick and effective decisions. Any iota of self doubt will never allow you trust the decision you take and that self doubt would be the biggest enemy of yours.

Your knowledge base forms another important pillar to your ability to take quick and effective decision, if there is no fact or knowledge backing your decisions, it might be a case of overconfidence rather than being in the illusion of confidence.

Liveliness:- Liveliness can be defined as a leadership quality that is characterised by energy, enthusiasm, and a positive attitude.

A lively leader is someone who brings a sense of vibrancy and vitality to their work and inspires others to do the same. They have a contagious energy that motivates their team to take action and tackle challenges with enthusiasm.

In a startup environment, where there are often long hours and many obstacles to overcome, liveliness is a valuable quality. A lively leader can help to boost morale and keep the team focused on their goals, even during tough times. They are often able to inject energy into the team and keep them engaged and productive.

Lively leaders are also typically good at building relationships and networking. They are outgoing and personable, and they are able to connect with people on a personal level. This can be particularly valuable in a startup environment, where networking and relationship-building are often critical to success

Lively leaders also have the ability to think outside the box and come up with creative solutions to problems. They are often able to generate new ideas and perspectives, which can help to move the startup forward. They are often able to inspire others with their enthusiasm and creativity, which can be a great asset to any startup.

In addition to all these qualities, lively leaders also tend to be good at managing stress and adapting to change. They are often able to remain focused and motivated even when faced with difficult and unpredictable situations. This can be hugely beneficial in a startup environment, where change is often a constant.

Liveliness is a state of mind that you must practice avoid you as well as your team do not have the feeling of burnout due the burden of the challenges faced on a constant basis. Practicing meditation, playing sports along with your team and practicing a positive frame of mind would help you to stay lively in difficult situations. Do not let worry and fear control your day-to-day activities, they must be driven by passion and love for what you have chosen to do, in doing so you will be able to bring energy and enthusiasm to the group.

Raising a new startup right from the ground is undoubtedly a tough task, it is expected for the team to undergo a pressure. Hence it becomes even more important, when your team would be working really hard, as a result you must be able to motivate and inspire the team, the ability to think outside the box and come up with creative solutions. You must be able to make the work environment enjoyable and foster a sense of camaraderie among the team.

Factor four: Dynamic

Factor four focuses on another important aspect of leadership that is the ability to have dynamic qualities to be a successful leader. Let's take a closer look at each of these qualities.

Having a Dynamic personality is the ability to adapt to changing situations and think on your feet. Having a dynamic attitude will help you to stay agile and responsive to changes in the market, which will help you to stay ahead of your competition. This includes qualities like determination, courage, and stamina. These are essential qualities for any leader to have, as they will help you to keep the team focused on your goals and keep them motivated to reach there.

Determination:- Determination is key for any leader. Determination is the ability to remain focused and motivated, even when facing difficult challenges. It is the ability to stay committed and driven even when the going gets tough. Having a determined attitude will help you to stay focused and reach your goals. It will also help you to stay positive and resilient when times are tough.

A leader who is determined to succeed will focus on the task at hand and stay committed to achieving their goals. They will also be able to identify opportunities and take advantage of them to further their success. They will be able to look past any setbacks and continue to strive towards their goals.

Determination is also important when it comes to dealing with failure. When you are determined you will be able to look at failure as an opportunity to learn and grow. You will be able to use failure as a learning experience and move on from it.

How determined you are will depend on the reason behind why you chose to start the food business and why you have the certain goal to achieve. Just a mere thinking that I want to make a certain amount of money might not be a strong motivator, instead it's advisable to have a emotional reason behind why you want to reach a certain goal, as a result every failure will further strengthen your determination to reach your goal.

As the founder of a startup, you must have the determination to make it a success, no matter what obstacles you face. This will help you stay motivated and stay on track towards achieving your goals. It is important to have a clear vision of what you want to achieve and to stay focused on the task at hand.

Courage :- It is the ability to take risks and put yourself out there, even when it is uncomfortable. It is the ability to stand up for what you believe in and take action, even when it is difficult.

Having courage will help you to push boundaries and take calculated risks in order to achieve your goals.

Leaders with courage are also willing to admit when they have made a mistake. You must not be afraid to take responsibility for your actions and learn be willing to learn from your mistakes. This will further strengthen your sense of responsibility and greatly increase your credibility in the eyes of the team. You will be amazed to see how much your team trusts and relies on you.

You must understand that mistakes can be a learning opportunity, and that it is important to be open to learning and growing as a leader.

As the founder of a startup, you must have the courage to make difficult decisions and to take risks. This will help you stay on top of the competition and be successful in the long run.

Stamina:- Having stamina as a startup founder is essential to withstand failures and continue to strive for success. Stamina refers to two different aspects an individual.

a) Physical stamina
b) Mental stamina

Physical stamina is the ability to maintain physical exertion over a long period of time. It is a critical factor for success in a variety of tasks, especially those that require sustained effort. A startup founder needs physical stamina in order to withstand the long hours and intense work that comes with running a business.

Physical stamina can help you to stay focused during long days and nights of work, remain energised through difficult tasks, and remain motivated when the going gets tough. It can also help you to stay healthy, as physical activity is an important part of staying fit and avoiding burnout.

Physical stamina also helps with decision making and problem solving. It can provide the mental clarity needed to make difficult decisions, and it can help you to stay in control when things become stressful. When times are tough, physical activity can be a great way to blow off steam and regain focus.

Mental stamina Could be referred to the trait that answers the following questions

How do you perform under stress?

Can you keep your cool and keep a calm mind under tough times?

How long can you really endure continuous stress and work efficiently?

Can you really overcome your stress and deal with the situation?

Mental stamina again refers your minds abilities to keep going, It is much more important than physical stamina because it is the mental stamina that allows you to keep going even when your body has physically given up. The power of the mental stamina can do miracles to an individual's abilities. Just to give you a perspective, from my personal experience as well as from the experiences shared by my son from his cadet days, even the fittest cadets could run run only a few kilometres due to their physical stamina, post that it was the mental stamina that allowed everyone to continue and complete the run.

Developing your mental stamina will help you to work long hours in a high-pressure environment and to remain resilient in the face of stress and adversity.

This quality is particularly important when launching and nurturing a business, as it requires dedication, persistence, and the ability to push through difficult times. It is this kind of resilience and determination that can make the difference between failure and success.

These fifteen qualities are definitely the ones that you should focus on developing. Under the ideal conditions, Any leader must possess these qualities in order to be successful in his endeavour while leading a team, However it is human not to be perfect. You may not be able to perfectly develop all these qualities however the focus must be towards inculcating the discussed qualities by practicing them in the day to day lives.

You must understand the basic thing , the life in the startup is going to be very unpredictable, a path filled with challenges. Under these conditions leading a team is another challenge to overcome. Why we have deliberated so much about developing the leadership qualities is because your attitude will be the difference between a make or a break. If you possess the right attitude, you and your team will automatically find a way around any situation you will face.

On a longer run what will hold your business and your team together and inspire them to work harder to realise the dream you all have seen together is the attitude.

The individuals under your leadership would be observing you, your attitude and your behaviour from the day-to-day life. Your influential, responsible and positive attitude will give them the trust and the hope that it is possible to build the startup into a large successful company.

CHAPTER 9

The Food Production Setup

Consadering there are a lot of difficulties that any individual would have to take care of especially when trying to figure out from where and how the operations of this business will be run. The initial burden of the cost of setting up the operating space for the business might affect the finances of the family, especially for those without much savings.

Coming from a middle-class family there is one thing that is amply clear When it comes to money the savings in our FD or in the mutual fund are the only support that we have. Spending huge sums of money is a big deal for us. Investing large sums of money into risky assets make us uncomfortable. Irrespective of the financial conditions almost every household has one asset which is the kitchen.

Your kitchen-based food startup is the perfect solution to start off your business without Putting much pressure on your pocket. Being the cheapest alternative to start your business, You also do not have to leave the comfort of your home. This can be an exciting and rewarding venture especially when you see the sales growing exponentially alongside being able to spend your time with the family and the kids. This venture is sure to change your life provided you have done solid research on the market you plan to target along with immaculate planning.

Without a carefully planned food production setup, your young business may face various challenges, such as inconsistent product quality, food safety issues, low productivity, and increased costs. These challenges can not only impact the bottom line but also damage the reputation and credibility of the business.

On the other hand, a well-planned food production setup can lead to a range of benefits, such as increased efficiency, better product quality, reduced waste, and improved customer satisfaction. It will also help your business to comply with food safety regulations and achieve certifications that can open up new markets and opportunities.

In this chapter, we will explore the importance of a carefully planned food production setup and the key considerations and steps involved in creating one.

As a part of planning, you will have to make certain purchases and make some very important changes at your space to start your food startup operations.

First and foremost, you'll need to find ways to convert your existing place into a commercial kitchen. This is where all the food preparation and cooking will take place, and it should be equipped with the necessary tools and appliances.

A commercial kitchen includes an oven, stovetop, refrigerator, sink, and other appliances. You'll also need utensils such as pots, pans, and other cooking tools.

The next important piece of equipment you'll need is food storage. This can range from refrigerators and freezers to dry storage cabinets and shelves. You'll need to have enough storage to hold all the ingredients you'll need for your recipes. This is especially important if you'll be selling food products like baked goods or pre-prepared meals. This will essentially prevent your Food from cross-contamination and also keep it fresh for a longer duration.

In addition to a commercial kitchen and food storage, you'll also need to invest in some basic cooking equipment. This includes a food processor, blender, mixer, and other kitchen appliances. These are essential for creating delicious dishes and desserts.

You'll also need to purchase some good quality utensils such as knives, cutting boards, measuring cups, and more bases on the food products you plan to sell.

These are just some of the basic pieces of equipment you'll need to start your food business smoothly. Yet it's important to remember that running a food business also comes with a certain set of risks. To ensure the safety of your customers as well as your loved ones at home, it's essential to invest in the right safety equipment.

Food safety is essential for any food business, and running a business from home is no exception. It will be your responsibility for ensuring that the food you will be producing is safe and healthy for consumption. You should take the time to learn about food safety practices and adhere to them. This includes washing your hands thoroughly before handling food, keeping food at the right temperature, and avoiding cross-contamination.

Needless to say, make sure to use only clean utensils and equipment when preparing food. It is advisable to have a pair of gloves and a face mask to ensure both good hygiene and also to guard against any spills or messes.

The most important piece of safety equipment for running a food business from home is all the kitchen equipments should be in good working condition and should be regularly cleaned to ensure proper hygiene, and obliviate any chances of the equipment malfunctioning leading to any kind of a compromise in the safety of the individuals working inside the kitchen. This is the cheapest but the best way to ensure a healthy and safe environment in your kitchen.

Since the quality and the safety of the food produced greatly depends on the temperatures, get a thermometer to monitor the temperature of food products. It is important to understand that the different foods need to be cooked to different temperatures to be safe for consumption.

You must also consider installing a fire extinguisher. This is especially important if you're using an oven, stove, or any other type of open flame as these items are more prone to fire-related accidents. Fire extinguishers should be placed in an easily accessible location. Make sure to inspect the fire extinguisher regularly to ensure it's in a safe and working condition.

As a part of basics, a first aid kit is a part of every household and must be kept handy in case of any small accident such as accidental cuts or burns which are very common to happen while working in the kitchen. This should include all the basic first aid items such as bandages, antiseptic wipes, pain relievers, ice packs etc.

While the list may sound long however most of these equipment's would be already available at home. Once your list is ready you may realise that you're just a few purchases away from completing the set-up required to get started with the product development process.

However, it's not just important to purchase equipment's and setup the home food production setup but also organising your home kitchen makes the difference to help you to get the most out of your space and time.

Start with a clean slate, before you can organise your kitchen, you need to start with a clean and clutter-free space. Take everything out of your cabinets and drawers, and give all the corners a good scrub. This will also be a good time to declutter and get rid of any items that you no longer need or use. Divide your kitchen into zones based on the functions. For example, create a baking zone, a prep zone, a cooking zone etc. This will help you to work more efficiently by keeping all of your tools and ingredients in one place.

Don't forget about your vertical space! utilising the vertical space will allow you to generate and use extra space. Install some shelves, hooks and racks to make the most out of your wall space. This is the best way to store items that you use frequently such as pots and pans, utensils and spices.

make sure to Group similar items together. Keep all of your baking tools and ingredients together and all of your cooking tools and ingredients together. This will make it easier to find what you need and work more efficiently.

Label everything in your kitchen, labelling your containers, shelves and drawers can save your precious time and reduce stress. Use a label maker or masking tape and a marker to label everything, from your spice jars to your storage containers.

Keep the items you use most often within your easy reach. This might include your favourite spatula, your go-to spice blend, or your trusty mixing bowl. This will help you work more efficiently and reduce frustrations.

Invest in good quality storage containers, good-quality storage containers can help you keep your ingredients fresh and organised. Look for airtight containers with clear labels to make it easy to see what's inside.

Make use of drawer dividers, Drawer dividers can help you keep your utensils and tools organised and easy to find. They're also a great way to make the most of your drawer space.

Use a whiteboard or a chalkboard, A whiteboard or chalkboard can be a great way to keep track of your to-do list, shopping list, and recipe ideas. Hang one up in your kitchen and use it to stay organised and on track.

the last thing is that the best ways to stay organised and productive in the kitchen is to clean as you go. Wash dishes and utensils as you use them, and wipe down surfaces and spills as soon as they happen. This will help you stay away from piling up of messes and reduce stress.

The most important thing to bear in mind is to make sure that you have all the necessary types of equipment to ensure that once your business starts it's fully prepared to run smoothly and successfully.

CHAPTER 10

Preparing the Signature Food

Product of the Startup

I t is now the time to create a signature food product for the food

startup. A signature product is going to be the centrepiece of your brand. If it is done correctly, it will be the game changer, it's the dish that your customers will remember and crave for, the one they'll tell their friends about, and the one that will keep them coming back for more. This will be a major element that will set you apart from your competition, it's going to be the identity of your business.

Most entrepreneurs launching a food product, dream of making it a success. But the reality is that many of these products fail to gain traction in the marketplace. Developing a successful food product requires a great deal of skill, knowledge, and hard work. we'll discuss the key skills and steps required to create a successful food product.

It is extremely important to take the necessary steps to ensure the product is of high quality and meets the needs of your potential customers. Whether you are an experienced chef or a novice, it is important to keep things simple.

Though you may have an understanding that food businesses required a large set of menus and food products to be successful the reality is quite the opposite. Don't try to create a large menu with a variety of items. Instead, focus on a few core items that can be easily prepared and served quickly. This will help to keep costs down and make it easier to manage production leading into a more efficient business.

Take out your research work, and refer to the details of the data and the conclusions drawn from it. Now consider the type of product you plan to develop. after finally Deciding who you are targeting, and what is that unique thing you plan to have in your final product. It is important to think about how you can differentiate your product from similar products on the market. Think about the flavours it will have, and what kind of unique textures and ingredients you want to include to make your product stand out.

It's not enough to simply follow a recipe; ask the team to think, there is a need to use everyone's imagination and creativity to come up with something truly unique. Think about how different ingredients can be combined to create something special. Consider how flavours and textures can be combined to create something that tastes unique as well as amazing.

Use your creativity to come up with something that's truly your own. It's important to pay attention to the details. Every ingredient should be measured accurately, and instructions should be followed precisely. A single mistake has the ability to change the entire outcome of the recipe, so it's important to make sure that everything is done correctly. Paying attention to the details also ensures that the recipe is well documented and can be exactly replicated every time in future.

You need to develop an understanding of how different ingredients interact and how they will affect the outcome of the recipe. You also need to learn and understand the different cooking techniques and how they can be used to create something truly delicious. Cooking techniques are an essential part of any cook's repertoire.

Knowing which techniques to use and when can these techniques make the difference between a dish that's just okay and one that's truly delicious.

No matter what type of dish you're making, understanding the different cooking techniques and how they can be used to create something truly delicious can help you develop your signature product.

The next big factor is Practice. Practice makes a man perfect, and this is especially true when it comes to developing that perfect product your team is planning to make. If a recipe is prepared many times, it will be directly proportional to accuracy. It's important to experiment with different ingredients and techniques in order to refine your skills. Don't be afraid to try something new; it's the only way to learn and improve. Creating a successful food recipe can be a long and challenging process.

It may take several attempts to get it just right, so it's important to be patient. Don't give up if something doesn't work out the first time; keep tweaking and experimenting until you get it right, however keep one important point in mind while you plan and work towards developing the food product, this especially applies to those businesses which have tight budget and look forward to scale the business to a greater extent.

Create a food product with a good shelf life and easy to package, food products or dishes those needs be consumed within a few hours has its drawbacks.

The most obvious one is that they are not as convenient as food that can be stored and consumed at a later time. This means that the food must be prepared, served, and eaten within a few hours, or it will not be edible. This will limit your business to just your locality, you won't have the option to scale it to a large scale. In order to scale the business to a large scale, it will demand huge investment.

A food product with a good shelf life and can be easily packaged can be produced in large quantities and sold on a larger scale, making it easier for your startup to grow and expand. This means you can reach more customers and increase your revenue.

Another major disadvantage of developing food products that must be consumed within a few hours is that they are more expensive. Preparing a meal that must be consumed within a few hours requires more ingredients, as well as more time, energy, and effort.

This means that the cost of producing the food is higher significantly, not only from product point of view but also the daily cost of running the business is huge. You will have to hire more people necessary to quickly prepare, package, and deliver the product to customers leading to more salaries to pay!

On the other hand, developing food products with a longer shelf life helps to reduce the cost of running the business significantly, it helps reducing the cost of labour, as fewer employees are needed to manage the inventory of food items which helps businesses to better manage their cash flow, as they don't have to worry about replacing outdated food items as often.

It can also help businesses to better manage their marketing efforts, as they can plan and execute promotions more effectively, knowing that their products will helps to reduce the cost associated with product spoilage, as the food can be stored and consumed for a longer period of time.

The short shelf life of the food products is less convenient for customers as well. Customers may be reluctant to buy foods that have a short shelf-life, as they may be uncertain of their freshness or quality. Furthermore, customers may not have the time or resources to consume the product within the specified timeframe.

Customers today are looking for convenient food options that fit their busy lifestyles. A food product with a good shelf life and easy packaging allows them to grab your product on-the-go and enjoy it at their convenience, whether it's for a quick snack or a full meal.

A food product with a good shelf life allows for longer storage times, reducing the risk of spoilage and waste. This not only saves money for the business but also helps to reduce food waste, which is an important environmental concern.

It also allows for greater consistency in quality, which is important for building a loyal customer base. Customers want to know they can rely on your product to taste the same every time they purchase it, even a slight variation in taste, smell or texture in the product may cost you the loyalty of the customer base that you will build over a long period of time.

Now once you feel that you have a product which you can launch, wait it's time to take some valuable feedback, gather some of your friends and family, offer them this unique food product that you have created, everyone loves a free meal, so it's not going to be difficult to gather them as well as this can be a great time to spend with them. Give them the time to enjoy your product, Now take valuable feedback from them, What they liked about your food product what they did not like about the food product, What kind of changes and variations they would love to see in future, Note them down and then work on it, Once you feel again you have the product ready with the necessary changes, offer them once again To understand if they like it and whether It is the change in the product that they had desired to see.

It will even be smarter to gather a small section of your target audience and repeat the same process, after all the aim is that the product is liked by the target audience. Gather all the feedback's and work on it, these valuable feedback's will allow you to develop and improve your food product that suits your target audience, however don't overdo it.

If you aim to satisfy everyone's expectations, you may end up exhausting a lot of your resources and time and still you may not be able to fully satisfy everyone's expectations. The aim is to improve, not aim for perfection, hence this process of utilising feedback's will definitely help you develop an amazing food product.

With the right combination of creativity, attention to detail, and knowledge of food science and techniques, you can create something unique and delicious. With a bit of practice, patience and smartly utilising the feedback's, you can create the final signature food product ready to be launched in the market.

CHAPTER 11

The Power of Attractive Packaging and Building a Brand for Your Food Product Launch

I

t is finally the moment of launching a food product and no doubt this is a big step for your business. It's a time of excitement and anticipation, as well as a time of risk and uncertainty. But there's one thing that can help ensure the success of your food product launch: attractive packaging and building a strong brand.

When it comes to food products, the packaging can be just as important as the product itself. A well-designed package can be the difference between a product that stands out from the crowd, and one that gets lost in the shuffle. Good packaging has the ability to draw the eye of potential customers, prompting them to take a closer look, and it also communicates the quality as well as the value of the product, giving customers the confidence to go ahead and try your product. In simple terms it is fair to say what is visible will sell, what is not visible won't. No matter how good your product is, it has to be visible first to your target audience. That's exactly what this step will do for your product.

But how can companies create a package design that stands out from the competition?

Here are some tips for creating a well-designed package that will draw customers in and give them the confidence to make a purchase.

First, it's important to consider the product itself when designing the package. You need to answer the questions while thinking of well-designed packaging.

What are the unique features of your product?

What are the unique benefits of the product? (Remember a feature mainly refers to the facts of your food product however the benefits help to connect your consumers to your product on an emotional level.)

Does it have a unique shape or size?

Does it have a unique colour or texture?

All of these elements should be taken into consideration when creating the package design. The package should be designed to emphasise the product's unique features, while also strongly communicating the brand's unique identity.

It's also important to consider the customer's needs when designing the package. The following questions would help you determine that easily

What are the customer's expectations when it comes to the product?

What type of package will be best suited to meet those expectations?

The most important thing to understand is that the package should be designed to meet the customer's needs

Another important thing to consider is the customer's lifestyle when designing the package.

Does the customer lead a busy lifestyle? If so, the package should be designed to be easy to open and close.

Does the customer have young children? If so, the package should be designed to be child-proof.

Make sure to show this as an added benefit of the product, so that

those features do not go unnoticed by your target audience.
Next, it's important to consider the environment when designing the package.

What type of material should be used to create the package?

Is the package recyclable or biodegradable?

Is the package designed to be reused or repurposed?

All of these elements should be taken into consideration when creating the package design. The package should be designed to be as eco-friendly as possible, while also communicating the brand's identity. This will further attract a small section of environment-friendly community towards your product and further play a major role in helping your product to stand out in the market.

At last, it's important to consider the packaging process when designing the package.

What type of printing process should be used?

Is the package designed to be shipped or stored?

All of these elements should be taken into consideration when creating the package design. The package should be designed to be as cost-effective and efficient as possible, without compromising the brand's quality as well its identity.

When it comes to packaging, simplicity is often the best option available. Keep the design clean and straightforward, and make sure the most important information is easy to find.

Of course, the most obvious objective of the packaging should be that it is designed to protect the product from damage and maintain its freshness. Use high-quality materials that will protect the product and make it look its best.

But packaging isn't the only factor in a successful food product launch. Building a strong brand is also essential. A good brand is essential for any business to have its unique identity, regardless of size. It is more than just a logo and a catchy name; it's about creating an emotional connection with your customers.

It should evoke feelings of trust and loyalty. It takes time, effort, and dedication. But when done correctly, it can create an emotional connection with customers that will last for years to come.

When it comes to branding, what are the several elements that must be taken into consideration?

The first, and perhaps most important, is the logo. The logo is a visual representation of the company and it should be designed with the company's values and mission in mind. It should be recognisable and memorable, and it should be used consistently across all of the company's marketing materials.

The next element of a good brand is the company's mission statement. This should be a concise explanation of the company's goals and objectives. It should be clear and concise, and it should be used consistently across all of the company's marketing materials.

The third element is the company's slogan or tagline. This should be a memorable phrase that captures the essence of the company's mission and values. It should be used consistently across all of the company's marketing materials.

The fourth element is the company's brand identity. This should be a consistent look and feel for all of the company's marketing materials. This includes the logo, the mission statement, the slogan or tagline, and any other visuals such as colours, fonts, and images.

The fifth element is the company's tone of voice. This should be a consistent tone that is used across all of the company's marketing materials. It should be friendly, professional, and engaging.

The sixth element is the company's content. This should be engaging and informative, and it should be used consistently across all of the company's marketing materials.

The seventh element is the company's customer service. This should be friendly, helpful, and responsive. It should be used consistently across all of the company's marketing materials.

Finally, the eighth element is the company's customer loyalty program. This should be designed to incentivise customers to purchase from the company. It should be used consistently across all of the company's marketing materials.

When it comes to creating an emotional connection with customers. It takes a combination of all of the elements listed above. It takes consistency across all of the company's marketing materials. It takes a commitment to provide great customer service. And it takes a loyalty program that rewards customers for their continued patronage.

Your packaging and branding should work together to create a unified look and feel that's both attractive and informative.

One of the most important things to consider when designing a package and brand is the target audience.

Who are you trying to reach with your product?

What do they care about?

What do they need to know about your product?

Answering these questions will help you create packaging and branding that speaks to the needs of your target market. You

should also consider the competition. What do other food

products in your category look like?

How can you make your product stand out?

Answering these questions will help you create packaging and branding that will make your product stand out from the competition allowing your customers to identify your product. don't forget to include your branding on the package; this will help customers recognise your product and create a strong connection with your brand.

Attractive packaging and strong branding can make a big difference in the success of your food product launch.

Though this sounds very expensive however the good news is that creating an attractive package and a strong brand doesn't have to be difficult or expensive at all.

With the right strategy and a bit of creativity, you can create a package and brand that will make your product stand out from the crowd. So don't forget to give your packaging and branding the attention they deserve.

CHAPTER 12

Legalities and Obtaining the Essential Licenses

S o finally, you are clear about the product that you are going

to sell, you have your team in place and the basic setup is complete as well from where you are ready to launch the food product that you have developed. However, before rushing towards the sales and marketing of the product it's important to obtain the necessary licenses to stay away from any kind of legal troubles.

This is necessary because the food industry is a highly regulated industry. In order to ensure that food products are safe for consumption, governments have put in place a set of rules and regulations that must be followed. It is essential for food producers to be aware of these regulations and to ensure that their products meet all requirements.

This includes obtaining the necessary permits, licenses, and health and safety certificates. It is also important to ensure the product is properly labelled and meets the nutritional requirements of the target market. Food producers must ensure that the product is properly labelled, including any allergen information, nutrition facts, and expiration dates.

The labelling of food products is a legal requirement in most countries and is designed to ensure that consumers are able to make informed decisions about the food they are purchasing.

These Labels are also used to provide information about the nutritional content of food products. This includes the amount of calories, fat, protein, carbohydrates, and other nutrients contained in each serving size. This information is important for those who need to monitor their dietary intake, or who have specific dietary needs due to medical conditions.

It must provide information about the freshness of food items. This includes the "best before" date, which indicates how long the food can be stored safely before it should be discarded. This information is important for food safety and quality control.

Proper labelling is also an important marketing tool, as consumers are more likely to purchase products that are clearly labelled and contain the necessary information. When designing labels, manufacturers should consider the size and shape of the label, as well as the type of font and colour used. Labels should be designed to stand out, as this will help to ensure that consumers are able to identify the product quickly and easily.

The first step in ensuring that a food product meets all regulations is to obtain the necessary permits and licenses. These permits and licenses are issued by government agencies and must be obtained before beginning the production process.

Depending on the type of product being produced and the country in which it is being manufactured, different permits and licenses may be required. It is important to research the applicable regulations to ensure that all requirements are met.

In addition to obtaining the necessary permits and licenses, food producers must also ensure that their products meet all health and safety requirements. This includes ensuring that the product is free from any contaminants and is manufactured in a sanitary environment.

It must be your endeavour to ensure that the product meets the nutritional requirements of the target market. This includes ensuring that the product contains the required nutrients, vitamins, and minerals. Additionally, the product should be low in sodium, sugar, and saturated fat. It is also important to ensure that the product follows the rules and regulations with respect to the use of any artificial flavours or preservatives.

By ensuring that a food product meets all regulations and requirements for food production, food producers can ensure that their products are safe and nutritious. they can be confident that their products will meet the needs of their target market. Taking the time to ensure that all regulations and requirements are met can help to ensure the success of any food product.

If you are operating your business in India, you should be aware that the food industry in India is regulated by the Food Safety and Standards Authority of India (FSSAI), which is an autonomous body established under the Ministry of Health and Family Welfare. The FSSAI is responsible for setting standards and regulations for food safety, ensuring that all food produced in India is safe and of the highest quality. It also works to promote public health and nutrition and is responsible for the regulation of food businesses, including production, storage, distribution, and sale.

In order to ensure that food produced in India is safe, FSSAI has implemented a number of regulations. These include the Food Safety and Standards Act, of 2006, which sets out the general principles for food safety and hygiene, as well as the Food Safety and Standards (Licensing and Registration of Food Businesses) Regulations, of 2011, which require food businesses to obtain a licence from the FSSAI.

In addition, FSSAI has also introduced several other regulations, such as the Food Safety and Standards (Packaging and Labelling) Regulations 2011, which sets out the requirements for food packaging and labelling. It also requires that food businesses provide consumers with accurate and up-to-date information about the ingredients and nutritional value of their products. Furthermore, FSSAI has also introduced regulations on food additives and contaminants, as well as food hygiene and sanitation.

Furthermore, FSSAI also works with state governments to ensure that food safety standards are implemented and enforced. This includes the establishment of food testing laboratories and the appointment of food safety officers.

In addition to the regulations set by FSSAI, the food industry in India is also regulated by various other laws, such as the Essential Commodities Act, of 1955, which regulates the production, distribution, and sale of essential commodities. The Prevention of Food Adulteration Act, of 1954 also sets out the standards for food safety and ensures that food is not adulterated.

Now, not just from the point of view of the laws in India but also all around the globe, It can be a challenge to keep up with the ever-changing regulations, but there are several reliable methods you can use to stay informed.

Regularly reviewing all relevant industry publications and attending conferences or workshops are two of the most reliable ways to stay up to date with the latest laws. Industry publications can provide invaluable insight into the current legal landscape, and attending conferences and workshops can give you access to experts who can provide the latest information on changing laws, as well as these activities will actually help you in all aspects related to building yourself and your business in the food industry

Another effective way to stay informed of changes in the law is to consult with a lawyer or consultant from time to time. This can be especially beneficial for businesses that operate in multiple jurisdictions, as the laws may vary from state to state or country to country. Consulting with a professional will ensure that you are aware of all the applicable laws and regulations that apply to your business.

staying connected to other business owners and professionals in your industry is a great way to stay informed of changes in the law. Networking with others in your field can give you access to the latest information and insights into any changes that may affect your business.

it's important to remember that the law is constantly changing and evolving, in certain countries the changes are more frequent than others. in few countries the law changes from one state to another, utilising these fail-proof methods do allow your Situational awareness to increase and have the necessary informations handy.

Overall, food production in India is highly regulated in order to ensure that the food produced is safe and of the highest quality.

As a food producer, it is essential to ensure that your product meets all the regulations and requirements for food production. This includes having a clear understanding of the relevant laws and regulations and making sure that your product is safe to consume. It is important to have appropriate controls in place to ensure that you are producing a safe product, and to have a plan in place to deal with any issues that may arise.

It is important to have a quality assurance system in place to ensure that your product meets the highest standards of quality. By following these guidelines, you can ensure that you are providing a safe, high-quality product to your customers.

-CHAPTER 13-

Producing a Food
Product on a Large
Scale the Smart Way

O nce a food product has been developed, the next step is to manufacture it on a large scale to meet consumer demand. This is a complex process that requires careful planning and execution. From selecting the right equipment to establishing a reliable supply chain, there are many factors to consider to ensure a successful launch.

The first thing is to select the right production equipment. The type of equipment needed will depend on the type of product being produced. For example, if the product is a baked good, a commercial oven and other baking equipment may be needed. If the product is a beverage, a bottling machine and other related equipment may be required. It is important to select equipment that is reliable, efficient, and cost-effective. By now you already have your home setup available based on the product you have successfully made hence these needs are already taken care of.

Once the right equipment has been selected, it is important to ensure that it is properly maintained and serviced to ensure optimal performance.

Not it is the time to establish a reliable supply chain. Find the right suppliers for the ingredients and packaging materials needed for the product. It is important to select suppliers that are reliable and can provide quality ingredients and materials at a reasonable cost. It is also important to establish a good relationship with the suppliers to ensure a steady supply of ingredients and materials.

Once the equipment and supply chain are in place, next develop a production process. This includes creating a workflow that is efficient and cost-effective. It is important to consider factors such as the number of batches needed, the time it takes to produce each unit, and the cost of materials. It is also important to create systems for quality control and product traceability to ensure that the product meets all safety and quality standards. You may consider outsourcing some of the processes to reduce the workload. It is important to work smart more than to work hard.

Outsourcing is a popular and effective way to reduce the workload of a production team. Undoubtedly it is a great way to reduce costs and increase efficiency. By outsourcing certain processes, your production team can focus on core activities while allowing an external provider to manage non-core tasks. This can be advantageous in many different ways, from reducing labour costs and improving quality to providing access to specialised skills and resources.

The most obvious benefit of outsourcing is cost savings. Outsourcing certain processes to external providers can help to reduce labour costs, as the provider can often offer a lower rate than an in-house team. outsourcing can also help to reduce overhead costs, as the provider can handle the administrative and operational tasks that would otherwise be handled by the production team.

 By outsourcing certain processes, your company can also save money on training and equipment, as the provider typically already has the necessary resources and skills. Considering the small size of the team you have with you, the maximum focus needs to be on the sale, development, marketing, customer acquisitions and growth of the company rather than trying to run everything in-house.

Outsourcing can also help to improve quality and consistency. By outsourcing certain processes to an external provider, your team can ensure that the products and services are up to the highest standards.

The provider can provide specialised expertise and resources that may not be available in-house, allowing the company to produce better-quality products and services. Being new in this field, the experience may not be much at handling large-scale productions. outsourcing can help to reduce the risk of errors, as the provider can provide a consistent and reliable service.

Another benefit of outsourcing is access to specialised skills and resources. By outsourcing certain processes, your team can access specialised skills and resources that may not be available in-house. This can help to improve the quality of the products and services, as the provider can often provide better expertise and resources than an in-house team. As a new startup, you and your team are trying to keep the costs to a minimum while trying to meet the demands of the consumers in time, outsourcing can provide access to specialised tools and technologies that can help to speed up the production process.

Outsourcing can help to improve efficiency and help you being the output to the required standards. By outsourcing certain processes, companies can free up the production team to focus on core activities. This can help to improve the overall efficiency of the production process, as the production team can focus on tasks that are more important and can add more value to the company. This can definitely provide access to resources and skills that can help to speed up the production process, allowing the company to produce more products and services in less time.

Keeping all the points in mind, you and the team may want to keep a fine balance between the large-scale production as well as the quality of the product without having to take a huge burden as well as take all the benefits of a huge production house at a very low cost.

CHAPTER 14

Set Up a Budget

A

ccounting may not seem like the most exciting part of launching a food business, but it can be the difference between success and failure. Establishing a budget is an essential step in preparing a plan for a food business, and it will help you determine the cost of starting and running your business. Taking the time to create a realistic budget will help ensure that your business is successful.

It's not enough to simply have a plan for the initial launch; you must also have a plan for the long-term financial health of your business. That's why it is so important to look at your budget from different time horizons when planning for the food business you are about to launch.

Without proper planning, a food business can quickly become overwhelmed by unexpected expenses, leading to financial difficulties in the future. Fortunately, by taking the time to look at your budget from different time horizons, you can ensure that your food startup is well-positioned for success.

You'll need to consider a variety of factors to ensure the success of your venture. One of the most important considerations of all is the financial health of your business. A well-crafted budget, with an eye to both the short-term and the long-term, it's also important to consider both fixed and variable costs. Fixed costs are expenses that remain the same regardless of the business's performance. Examples of fixed costs include rent, salaries, and utilities. Variable costs are expenses that fluctuate depending on the business's performance.

Examples of variable costs include advertising and materials. It is key to making sure your food startup is profitable and sustainable.

You'll need to ensure you're able to cover the cost of ingredients and other expenses related to setting up the business. You'll also need to account for marketing and other costs associated with launching the business.

When it comes to budgeting for the long-term financial health of your business, you need to look at your budget from different time horizons.

The first-time horizon to consider is short-term. This is typically a period of one to two years, and it's important to make sure your budget is able to cover your expenses for this period of time. This includes everything from ingredient costs to marketing expenses. It's important to consider how much startup capital is needed to get the business off the ground, what regular expenses need to be covered, and how much income is expected to be brought in. This type of planning can help ensure that the business has the resources it needs to get started and stay afloat during the initial stages.

It's also important to keep in mind that you may not be able to predict all of your expenses for this period of time, so it's important to have a cushion in your budget to account for unexpected costs.

The next time horizon to consider is the medium term. This is typically a period of three to five years, and it's important to make sure your budget is able to cover your expenses for this period of time. This includes everything from ingredient costs to marketing expenses, as well as any investments you may want to make in equipment or staff. It's also important to plan for any potential changes in the market or your business, as well as any potential changes in regulations or taxes that could affect your business.

Finally, you should also consider the long-term. This is typically a period of five to ten years, and it's important to make sure your budget is able to cover your expenses for this period of time.

It's important to consider how much money will be needed to sustain the business over the long term, what investments need to be made, and how much income is expected to be brought in. This type of planning can help ensure that the business has the resources it needs to continue to grow and be successful over the long term. It is also important to look at your budget from a strategic perspective. This means considering how much you are willing and able to invest in the long-term success of your business. For example, you may want to consider investing in research and development, which can help you create new and innovative products that will help your business stand out from the competition.

You may want to invest in marketing and advertising, both of which can help you reach new customers and spread the word about your business.

You may also want to look at your budget from a risk management perspective. This means considering the potential risks associated with launching and running a food business, such as the possibility of spoilage. By considering these potential risks, you can create a budget that will help you protect your business from financial loss in the event that one of these risks becomes a reality.

It's also important to consider both cash flow and profit when creating your budget. Cash flow is the amount of money coming in and out of the business. Profit is the amount of money that is left over after all expenses have been paid. It's important to consider both cash flow and profit when creating your budget, as this can help you determine how much money needs to be set aside for investments, taxes, and other expenses.

Invest the time to understand the short-term and long-term costs associated with launching and running a business, as well as the potential risks, by doing so you can ensure that your business is well-positioned for success. With a comprehensive plan in place, you can be confident that your food startup is on the right track for long-term financial health.

CHAPTER 15

Marketing the
Product

O nce the product concept has been identified, and everything in place to launch the business on a massive scale, entrepreneurs must develop a comprehensive marketing plan. Marketing is the pillar that effectively brings visible effects for the business attracting sales and customers.

Marketing is the lifeblood of any business. It is the process of creating awareness of a product or service and introducing it to potential customers. It is an essential part of any business, as it helps to create a competitive edge, attract more customers and increase sales.

Creating a comprehensive marketing plan for a food product is essential to ensure that once your product hit the market the sales are good in order to make good profits. The marketing plan is a document that outlines how a company will promote its product and reach its target audience. It should include objectives, strategies, tactics, and a timeline. A successful marketing plan is tailored for the product and its target audience and should be regularly monitored and adjusted to ensure that it is effective.

When developing a marketing plan for a food product, the first step is to identify the product concept. This means understanding the product's purpose, advantages, and target audience. From there, the marketing plan should be designed to reach the target audience and promote the product's advantages.

Once the product concept has been identified, the next step is to develop a comprehensive marketing plan. This plan should include Objectives, strategies, tactics, and a timeline.

The objectives should be specific and measurable and should reflect the overall goals of the product. First, objectives should be created that are in line with the ultimate goal of the product. For example, if the product is intended to increase customer engagement, objectives might include increasing the number of customer interactions or improving customer satisfaction ratings.

Once the overall goal is identified, objectives should be broken down into smaller, more measurable goals. These should be achievable, but also challenging. For example, if the goal is to increase customer engagement, objectives might include increasing the number of customer interactions by 10% in the next six months.

Objectives should also be aligned with the strategy and timeline of the product. They should be achievable within the allotted timeframe and should be flexible enough to accommodate any changes that may occur.

These objectives must be monitored and reviewed regularly. This will ensure that the product is on track and that any changes can be addressed quickly.
The strategies should be tailored for the product and its target audience, and should include both short-term and long-term goals and should be designed to ensure the product's success.

The short-term goals should focus on increasing brand awareness, driving sales, and reaching the desired target audience.

Long-term goals should include the process of Customer acquisition. It involves finding and converting potential customers into paying customers, building customer loyalty, improving customer experience, and creating a sustainable competitive advantage.

By creating an effective marketing strategy, businesses can ensure the success of their product and maximize their potential.

The tactics should be creative and cost-effective and should be designed to reach the target audience. Finally, the timeline should be realistic and achievable and should include regular check-ins to ensure that the plan is progressing as expected.
When creating a comprehensive marketing plan for a food product, it is important to consider the four P's of marketing: product, price, promotion, and place.

The product should be designed to meet the needs of the target audience and should be marketed accordingly.

The price should be competitive and should reflect the value of the product. Pricing should be based on market research and competitive analysis. It should also take into account factors such as cost of production, overhead, and other costs associated with the product or service.

The promotion has to be creative and should be designed to create awareness of the product or service and convince potential customers to buy it. Promotion may include advertising, public relations, sales promotions, and other activities.

Advertising should be targeted to the right audience and should focus on the benefits of the product or service.

Public relations is another way to promote a product or service. It involves creating relationships with the media, influencers, and other key stakeholders. Public relations can be used to build brand awareness and create positive sentiments about the product or service.

Sales promotions are another way to promote a product or

service. These are short-term activities designed to increase sales. Keep your focus on building a customer base. Examples of sales promotions include
offering discounts, coupons, or loyalty programs to attract customers

You should also focus on word-of-mouth marketing and creating relationships with local businesses.

The last P of the Ps stand for a place that is to find a location for the business. This can be a physical store, or it can be an online store. It is important to choose a location that is close to the target market, as this will make it easier to reach potential customers. Setting up a shop on a busy street or renting a place at a mall could do the trick, however, an online store would be the best and the most cost-effective option that I would suggest. There is a lot to discuss on this topic hence there is a detailed chapter dedicated to help you with regards to how one can make use of the technology as well as find the pocket-friendly solution.

At last Execution of all these plans would now be required to follow a timeline for the marketing plan. This timeline should be realistic and achievable and should include regular check-ins to ensure that the plan is progressing as expected.

The backbone of any business is marketing and sales, without sales there's no income or profit and so there is effectively no business. Hence by creating a comprehensive marketing plan for a food product, companies can ensure that their startup is profitable and successful. Hence, I would recommend you to focus well on the marketing the product.

CHAPTER 16

The Benefits of Selling Food Products Online

Selling food products online has become increasingly popular in recent years as an alternative to traditional expensive and high-maintenance stores. With the rise of e-commerce, selling food products online has become increasingly popular in recent years.

This trend has been driven by the convenience of online shopping, as well as the growing demand for speciality food items. As a result, more and more businesses are moving into the online space to take advantage of this trend. The food businesses are constantly looking to capitalise, using the various platforms available for selling food products online, such as Amazon, Flipkart, eBay, and other marketplaces.

The traditional method of setting up a shop or a store, these options come with their own drawbacks these methods require full-time attention and cannot be just a side hustle which can be done alongside the job which you are doing currently to support your family and meet the expenses till the time startup is up and running successfully.

Not just are these options expensive but also there is the risk of theft, as busy streets tend to attract more criminal activity. It can be difficult to keep the shop clean and tidy, as there will be a lot of foot traffic.

Another thing to consider is that it can be hard to keep the shop staffed, as it may be difficult to find trained staff as well as paying them all could be an expensive option,

Looking at the place to make sales from a return-on-investment point of view as well as an excellent result with respect to a lot of traffic and sales, the digital space will be the best bet to start with. what are the benefits of selling food products online?

Many entrepreneurs and small business owners are now leveraging the power of the internet to reach a larger, more diverse audience and increase their profits. The online marketplace provides a unique and cost-effective platform for selling food products, offering a range of benefits that are difficult to replicate in traditional stores.

One of the primary benefits of selling food products online is the potential to reach a wider audience. With an online store, you can reach customers all over the world, as opposed to a traditional store which is limited to the local area.

This means that you can reach customers from different countries and cultures, allowing you to expand your customer base and increase the potential for sales.

The internet allows customers to purchase products at any time of day, meaning that you can make sales even when your store is closed.

Another advantage of selling food products online is the cost savings associated with it. Setting up an online store is much less expensive than a physical one, as there is no need to rent or purchase a physical space.

The best part about the online store is that it has no additional costs, such as electricity, heating, or staff wages. This means you can keep your overhead costs to a minimum, allowing you to focus on growing your business.

One of the biggest advantages of selling food products online is the ability to customise the shopping experience for customers. You can tailor your website and store to meet the specific needs of your customers, allowing them to find exactly what they're looking for quickly and easily.

You can offer discounts and promotions to encourage customers to purchase from your store. This can help to increase customer loyalty and repeat business, allowing you to grow your business even more.

Selling food products online can also help to increase your visibility. Potential customers can easily discover an online store through search engines, social media, and other online platforms. This allows you to reach a larger audience and increase the potential for sales.

Take advantage of the technology, you may consider the use of digital marketing techniques such as SEO and social media marketing to increase your visibility further and reach more potential customers.

Selling food products online offer a range of advantages that make it an attractive option for entrepreneurs and small business owners. For these reasons, selling food products online is a great way to expand your business and maximise your profits and the options for doing so are vast.

You must understand the importance of marketing and branding and what difference can it make to your business, However, what happens when you have no one on your team with the experience or skills needed to market effectively?

When faced with a lack of experience or skills in the marketing department, it can be difficult to know what to do. The good news is that there are still ways to make sure your marketing efforts are successful, even if no one on your team has the necessary experience or skills. some options to consider to approach this challenge includes, hiring a Consultant, Outsourcing, Leveraging Technology, Investing in Training associated with marketing and sales.

The options that you may consider depends on a number of

factors such as your budget and the size of your team. There are chapters at the end of the book dedicated towards solving the similar problems in the most cost-efficient way.

But what do you do when no one from your team has the experience or skills needed to market effectively?

This question has been answered by the end of the book. Since this is a separate big topic in itself, it will be unwise to answer it in one or two paragraphs. As you read further, you will find that this concern has been addressed in detail.

CHAPTER 17

Shipping Your Food Product: Tips for Successful Delivery

O nce you've successfully launched a food product,

you've taken care of the packaging and branding, and you have a marketing plan in place, the next step is to ensure that you can get your product to your consumers.

Shipping your food product can be complicated, but you just need the right strategy in place, as a result you can ensure successful delivery and happy customers.

Shipping food products requires a specialised approach involving a combination of proper packaging, temperature control, and the right shipping partner.

Here are some tips that can help you ensure your food product is delivered to customers safely and on time.

1. Choosing the Right Packaging

Shipping food products can be a challenging endeavour. It is essential to make sure that your product is packed correctly and safely to ensure it arrives at its destination in the same condition in which it was sent. The first step in shipping your food product is to make sure you're using the right packaging. This will help ensure that your package is designed for the product you're shipping and that it's suitable for the shipping method you're using.

You want to ensure that your package is designed for the product you're shipping and that it's suitable for your shipping method. For example, if you're shipping a frozen food product, you may want to use an insulated shipping container to keep the product cold during transit.

If you're shipping a non-perishable food item, you may want to use a sturdy cardboard box, if you're shipping a fragile item, such as a cake or a pie, you'll need to use a box that's designed to protect the item during transit.

You should also consider the type of insulation you'll need to keep the product at the correct temperature during its journey. Additionally, you should select packaging that is easy to open and close, as well as easy to store and transport. Take due consideration about the materials which are better suited for certain types of products. For instance, if you're shipping a liquid product, you'll need to use a material that can contain the liquid without leaking.

In addition to the type of material, you should also consider the packaging size. You want to make sure that the packaging is large enough to fit the product but not so large that it takes up unnecessary space. Also, make sure that the packaging is lightweight and easy to carry. This will help reduce the cost of shipping, as well as make it easier to transport the product.

You also want to make sure that the packaging is designed to withstand the rigours of shipping. This means that the packaging should be able to withstand the elements, such as extreme temperatures, vibrations, and shocks. It's essential that the packaging should be able to protect the product from any potential damage that could occur during shipping.

2. Choose the Right Shipping Partner

The next step in shipping your food product is to choose the right shipping partner. You want to ensure that the shipping partner you choose is reliable and can provide the services you need. You also want to make sure that the shipping partner you choose is experienced in shipping food products and understands the unique challenges of shipping food items. Having the right partner can make the process much smoother. There are a few key things to consider when choosing a shipping partner for your food product.

First and foremost, you'll want to consider the partner's experience in shipping food products. Many shipping companies offer general shipping services, but not all of them specialise in food items. Be sure to ask potential partners if they have experience with shipping food products and if they can provide any unique services specifically for food items.

Pay attention to the reliability of the potential shipping partner. Shipping food products can be a time-sensitive process, so it's important to ensure that your partner can deliver on time. Ask potential partners about their track record for on-time delivery, and find out what kind of guarantees they can offer for timely delivery.

Pricing is another important factor to consider. Shipping food products can be expensive, so it's important to ensure that your partner can offer competitive rates. Ask potential partners for quotes, and then you should compare rates and services to ensure you're getting the best deal.

Pay attention to the partner's customer service. Having a reliable customer service team is essential when dealing with customer inquiries or issues that may arise during the shipping process. Ask potential partners about their customer service team, and find out what kind of support they can offer.

You'll want to consider the partner's technology. Many shipping companies offer online tracking and notifications, which can be helpful when it comes to keeping track of your shipments. Ask potential partners about their technology and find out what kind of tracking and notifications they can offer. Additionally, you should ensure that the shipping partner you choose is up-to -date on the latest regulations and laws governing food shipping, as this can help ensure that your product is shipped safely and legally.

3. Control Temperature

If you're shipping a food product that requires temperature control, you want to make sure that you're taking the necessary steps to keep the product at the right temperature during transit. This may involve using an insulated shipping container or special packaging materials to keep the product cool.

You must consider using a temperature-controlled shipping service, such as a refrigerated truck, to ensure that your product is kept at the right temperature during transit.

4. Consider Delivery Options

When shipping your food product, you want to make sure that you're offering your customers a variety of delivery options. This may include offering same-day, next-day, or even delivery in a specific timeframe. It's common to offer the options as per the costumers need, you may want to consider offering customers the option to pick up their orders from a local store or distribution centre.

5. Track Your Shipments

Make sure that you're tracking your shipments so that you can monitor their progress and ensure that they're delivered on time. This can help you stay on top of any potential delays and ensure that your customers are receiving their orders in a timely manner. tracking your shipments can help you identify any issues with the shipping process and take steps to resolve them quickly.

Shipping your food product carefully and on time can help you ensure successful delivery and happy customers as well as help your brand to earn the valuable trust and loyalty of your costumers. This will also enhance the value of your company and uplift the image for your company further.

CHAPTER 18

It is Time to Start Delegating Tasks

As a leader, it can be difficult to give up control and delegate tasks to your team. After all, you're the one responsible for the success of the team. However, delegating tasks is essential for success. It allows you to focus on the big picture and build a strong team.

Building a successful business takes time, and it can be a challenge to manage a team when you don't have the luxury of an office space. However, focusing on building trust and delegating tasks to your team in order to help your business grow is necessary.

Do you recall the question I asked you to consider while you were preparing the entrepreneur mindset

"If you had all the time and all the money in the world, what would you do?"

Well, if you don't learn to delegate tasks you might manage to earn a decent amount of money to afford a good lifestyle however you will never earn the time to enjoy the lifestyle, If you don't learn to delegate, your startup or business will never get automated, it will never run and grow without you and you will be forced to work hard throughout your life.

The story of my friend from Vadodara serves as an example of how important it is for entrepreneurs to understand the importance of delegation and the value of working with a team. It also serves as the example that even if you succeed alone, you won't reach too far alone no matter how well you do. Developing the habit of delegation and can help you create a more efficient and cost-effective business.

Delegation is not only important in terms of freeing up your time and energy, but it is also essential for the growth of your business. It allows you to scale your business by dividing the workload between multiple people. This will allow you to take on more projects, and increase your revenue.

Delegation is not just passing your job to someone else but it is the process of entrusting the team members with tasks based on their skills and abilities and expecting them to take the task with the same level of commitment as you would have given to the task.

It's a need rather than a luxury to delegate tasks in a way that allows team members to grow and develop their skills. This will help them to become more confident and competent in their roles.

Developing trust in your team should be your first priority. Trust is the foundation of any successful team, and without it, it can be difficult to move forward. To build trust, it is important to be open and honest with your team.

You need to trust that team members will do their best to complete the task. You also need to be willing to give up some control and let them take ownership of the task. This will help to build trust and create a strong team dynamic

Focus on communicating your expectations clearly and regularly and providing feedback in a constructive way. it is important to recognise each team member's strengths and weaknesses and offer support and encouragement when needed.

It's important to be clear about expectations. Make sure that team members understand what is expected of them and any deadlines that need to be met. It's also important to provide feedback and guidance throughout the process. This can be done by setting up regular check-ins with each team member, where they can provide updates on their progress. There has to be a system in place to provide feedback on their work in a timely manner.

Delegation can also help reduce the workload on you being the organisation leader. It can help to create a more productive and efficient workflow, as well as allowing you to focus on the bigger picture.

It will also allow the team members to take ownership of their tasks, which can help to boost morale and motivation and build a strong team.

While many of your teammates would be working very hard to make this startup a real success, make sure to reward and recognise your team's successes. This can be done through public recognition or other incentives. This will show your team that you value their hard work and will help to create a positive and productive work environment.

It's important to remember that delegation is a process. It takes time and practice to master. You may find yourself making mistakes along the way, but that's okay. As long as you're open to learning and improving, you'll be able to become a successful delegator and a successful leader.

CHAPTER 19

Be Smart with Finances

As a startup entrepreneur, managing your finances can be one of the most important aspects of running a successful business. A financial management system is a great way to help you stay organised and ensure that your finances are in order. A smart financial management system can help you run your startup more efficiently, save money, and make more informed decisions.

Having a financial management system in place can make the process more manageable. Without a system in place, it can be difficult to track income, expenses, and taxes, which can lead to costly errors and bad financial decisions. Failure to have a smart financial management system in place while running a startup can be a disaster.

Without a smart financial management system in place, a startup can quickly fall into disarray and may even be beyond repair and can have disastrous consequences.

One of the most common mistakes made by startups is failing to track their expenses and income. Without a good system in place, it can be difficult to keep track of where the money is going and where it is coming from. This can lead to mismanagement of funds, which can quickly put the startup in financial trouble.

Another common mistake is failing to budget properly. Without a budget, it can be difficult to plan for future expenses and to ensure that the startup has enough money to cover its expenses.

This can lead to cash flow shortages, which can be difficult to recover from.

Without a good financial management system in place, it can be difficult to secure funding. It can be difficult to demonstrate to potential investors that the startup is a good investment. Potential investors may be unwilling to invest in the startup without the necessary financial information.

Therefore, a smart financial management system must be in place before launching a startup.

The first step in creating a financial management system is to create a budget. This will help you track and manage your income and expenses. You can use a budget spreadsheet to track your income and expenses and set up categories for your spending. This will help you better understand where your money is going and how much you can afford to spend. Once you have a budget in place, you can start making informed decisions about allocating your resources.

The next step in creating a financial management system is to establish a system of accounts. You should have separate accounts for each source of income and expense. This will help you keep track of your finances and ensure that you are not overspending. You can also use these accounts to save for future investments or to pay off any debts.

Once you have your accounts set up, you can manage your finances. It is important to track your income and expenses and ensure you are not overspending. This can be done by creating a spreadsheet or using a financial software program. This will help you keep track of your finances and ensure you stay within your budget.

You should also make sure that you are setting aside money for taxes. This will help you stay compliant with the law and ensure that you are not overpaying or underpaying taxes. This can be done by creating a separate account for taxes or setting aside money each month to pay them

It is important to be smart about investments when it comes to being smart with the profit. This is especially true when it comes to ensuring healthy growth and availability of reserve funds on a longer horizon.

A sound financial strategy and investment plan can go a long way in helping a startup achieve its long-term goals. It is important to have a reserve fund to ensure that the startup has access to capital in the event of an emergency. This reserve fund should be managed carefully and should be replenished regularly.

An emergency fund should only be used for unexpected expenses. If you find yourself dipping into the emergency fund for everyday expenses, it's time to reassess your budget and cut back on spending.

You should make sure that you are creating a system for tracking investments. This will help you understand where your money is going and how it is being used. You can use investment tracking software to help you stay on top of your investments and make sure that you are making the right decisions.

By following these tips, startups can ensure that their finances and investments are managed in a way that maximises returns and minimises risk. This will help ensure that the startup has the resources it needs to grow and thrive in the long term.

CHAPTER 20

Outsourcing or Hiring Expertise: A Smart Business Move

I would like to congratulate you for having the patience to read through each and every chapter to understand all the steps and the processes that you and your team would have to go through to build a successful startup.

Though I intentionally decided to write about all the processes so that you know and understand the food sector in detail and plan the process of starting your venture with ease.

Having gone through so many detailed topics and detailed steps, I understand this must appear to you as a herculean task, I assure you that it is true however it is not as Herculean as it seems. The good news is there is a smarter way to run your business. You or your team would definitely not need to do each and everything on your own, this is a big mistake that most of the small-scale business attempt to do. However, this chapter will give you a smarter way out than most small and big successful businesses have been doing.

I definitely agree, for running a successful business, it is important to have the right expertise and resources available. However, it is not always possible to have the necessary expertise in-house, and this is where outsourcing or hiring expertise can be a smart business move.

Outsourcing or hiring expertise can help businesses to maximise their resources and focus on their core competencies. By leveraging outside resources and expertise, businesses can improve efficiency and reduce costs while also having access to the specialised skills they need.

But it is important to understand that outsourcing or hiring expertise is not a one-size-fits-all solution. It is important to carefully consider the needs of the business and the expertise required before making any decision. The businesses must ensure that they are properly supervising and focusing on what is needed, regardless of whether they are outsourcing or hiring expertise. In order to effectively supervise, there is a need for your team to have the core knowledge about each and everything that needs to be done so as to obtain the output you are looking for.

Let's explore how outsourcing or hiring expertise can be a smart business move and how businesses can ensure that they are getting the most out of the process.

Let us first focus on understanding about what is Outsourcing or Hiring Expertise.

Outsourcing or hiring expertise is the process of obtaining specialised skills and knowledge from outside sources. This could include hiring a consultant, freelancer, or other external providers to perform specific tasks or provide specific services.

The main advantages of outsourcing or hiring expertise are that businesses can access the specialised skills and knowledge they need without having to hire full-time staff. This can help businesses save money and reduce overhead costs. At the same time, the businesses can leverage the expertise of external providers who may have more experience and knowledge than the business itself.

When Should You Outsource or Hire Expertise?

Businesses should assess their needs when considering whether to outsource or hire expertise. If the business requires specialised skills or knowledge that they do not have in-house, then outsourcing or hiring expertise may be the best solution.

It is essential for businesses to consider the cost of outsourcing or hiring expertise. While there are savings to be made, businesses should also factor in the cost of managing and supervising the process.

How To Ensure You Are Getting The Most Out Of The Process

When outsourcing or hiring expertise, it is important to ensure that you are getting the most out of the process. This means that businesses must be clear about their expectations and ensure that they are supervising and focusing on what is needed.

When outsourcing or hiring expertise, businesses should create a clear plan and timeline for the project. This will help ensure that the project is completed on time and to the desired standards. Communicating what exactly is expected is important, businesses should ensure that there is effective communication between themselves and the provider, as this will help ensure that the project is completed to the highest standard.

Your team should make sure that they are properly monitoring the process. This means that businesses should track progress and provide feedback to ensure that the project is meeting their expectations.

These are the broad guidelines that need to be kept in mind while you make the smart move to outsource or hire expertise.

Based on the experience and the size of the team available, you may consider hiring or outsourcing expertise on several aspects such as when researching the business and sub-sector, planning or developing the food product, hiring a marketing team to take care of the marketing aspects and run your websites, or on server's other occasions you may encounter, remember to factor in these options as well. The idea is that the utilisation of this option could be a game changer for your food startup.

-CHAPTER 21-

Pay Yourself First

A

s an entrepreneur, it can be tempting to reinvest all of your profits back into your business. After all, your business is your passion, and the more you invest in it, the more likely it is to succeed. The good part is that you are undoubtedly aware of the importance of reinvesting profits back into the business. After all, reinvestment is the key to long-term growth.

As a result, it can be easy to get caught up in the excitement and forget to ensure that you are taking care of yourself financially. One of the most common mistakes that entrepreneurs make is forgetting to pay themselves first.

When starting a business, it can be easy to focus solely on the day-to-day operations. You may be so busy working on the business that you forget to pay yourself first. This can be a costly mistake. You need to make sure that you are taking care of yourself financially in order to ensure the success of your business.

As a business owner, you are investing your time, energy, and money into the business, and it is important that you prioritise your own financial well-being. It is a way of avoiding burnout and staying motivated to continue growing your business. This means setting aside a portion of your profits for your personal finances before you allocate money for other expenses.

The idea of paying yourself first is based on the principle of delayed gratification. Instead of spending all of your profits on current expenses, you're setting aside money for the future. This could be money that's invested in a retirement fund or in a savings account. It could also be money that's used to pay down debt or to invest in yourself by taking classes or investing in a business opportunity.

Start by setting aside money for yourself each month. In other words, set a salary for yourself as well as for each of your core team members. This can be a fixed amount each month, or it can be a percentage of profits. As your business grows, you should adjust your salary accordingly.

To be able to do this effectively, it's important to have a clear understanding of your business finances. You need to know exactly how much money is coming in, where it's going and regularly reviewing your financial statements to ensure that you're on track It's important to make sure that you're paying yourself a fair wage for the work you're doing.

This money should be used to cover your living expenses and any other financial obligations you may have. This action will acknowledge the value of your time and effort and ensures that you are able to support yourself and your family. It also creates a sense of financial security and stability that is necessary for the long-term success. After establishing your salary, you should set up a separate bank account for your personal finances. This will help you keep track of your spending and ensure that you're not dipping into your business profits for personal expenses.

you should also set up a reserve fund, this time it is your personal reserve fund, it's important to separate your business-related funds and personal funds as well as handle it separately. This personal reserve fund should be used for any unexpected expenses that may arise. Having a reserve fund will ensure that you are prepared for any financial surprises.

Another way to ensure that you are paying yourself first is to create a savings plan. This plan should include setting aside money for retirement, as well as for any other long-term goals you may have. Having a savings plan will help you stay on track with your short- and long-term financial goals and ensure that you are taking care of yourself financially.

It is important to remember that you are the most important asset to your business. You need to make sure that you are taking care of yourself financially in order to ensure the success of your business. Paying yourself first is a crucial part of being an entrepreneur, and it is essential that you prioritise your own financial well-being. By you I mean the team of all the Co-founders of the startup.

However, it's important to understand the concept that paying yourself first doesn't mean neglecting your business. You should still remember that the major portion of your profits back goes into the business to ensure its growth and success. This is the only way to ensure that your business can grow and become successful. By reinvesting your profits, you're able to reinvest in new equipment, hire additional staff, or even expand your business into new markets. All of these strategies can help ensure that your business is able to stay competitive and profitable in the long run.

While it is important to be compensated for your hard work, it is equally important to reinvest profits back into the business in order to ensure continued growth. So, the next time you're tempted to reinvest all of your profits back into your business, remember to pay yourself first.

CHAPTER 22

Balancing Act: The Importance of Maintaining a Healthy Lifestyle

C ongratulations, you've made it to the final chapter

of the book! Throughout this journey, we've explored the ins and outs of startup life, needed to succeed in the food industry, right from scratch to scale it to a good-sized profitable business, from the comfort of your homes. But as we come to the end of this book, it's important to reflect on a crucial aspect that's often overlooked: maintaining a healthy lifestyle.

The young startups and their founders face a unique set of challenges, from financial constraints and tight deadlines to constant pressure to innovate and grow. Well, that's how the world of startups is, where long hours of working, tight deadlines, and constant pressure are the norm.

Yes, it is exciting and greatly rewarding endeavour, it's important to be passionate and dedicated to your work, however it's equally crucial to maintain a healthy lifestyle in order to achieve long-term success.

In this chapter, we'll explore the importance of maintaining a balanced lifestyle, and provide actionable tips to help you prioritise your mental and physical health, and achieve sustainable success on both personal and professional front. So, whether you're a seasoned entrepreneur or just starting out, let's delve into the world of startup wellness and learn how to achieve a healthy "balancing act" in your life.

So, as you read through this final chapter, remember that the key to building a successful startup isn't just about working harder or longer hours - it's about taking care of yourself and building a sustainable foundation for success.

What is the need to maintain a balanced lifestyle?

Maintaining a balanced lifestyle is for critical for a number of factors, but to understand the importance of the question mentioned above, it's important to answer the next question

Do you want to attain good wealth by sacrificing your health and happiness?

We all want to be wealthy. We want to have enough money to pay for the things we want and to provide for our families. We're driven to make more money and to increase our wealth. But what happens when you get so focused on chasing wealth that you forget to take care of your health?

When you don't take care of your health, it can have serious consequences. Not only can it lead to physical and mental health issues, but it can also lead to financial problems. When you're not in good health, you may be unable to work, which can cause you to lose income. You may also be unable to take advantage of opportunities that arise, and you may need to pay for medical bills.

A lack of attention to your health can also lead to a lack of motivation. When you're feeling tired, overwhelmed, and unwell, it can be difficult to stay focused and motivated. This can lead to a decrease in productivity and a decrease in your income.

The most important thing to remember is that your health should always come first. Even if you're working hard and making money, it's important to take time to take care of yourself.

So, let's get back to answer the original question, we need to maintain balanced lifestyle for the following reasons

<u>For a good mental and physical health:</u>

When starting a business, entrepreneurs often take on a lot more than they can handle. The highs and lows of running a startup can be both exciting and overwhelming.

The demands of running a startup can be overwhelming. You will be responsible for all aspects of the business, from managing finances to hiring and training employees. You must also handle marketing, customer service, and more. This can be a lot to take on, and it can quickly lead to burnout.

Burnout is a state of physical, emotional, and mental exhaustion caused by prolonged or intense stress. Common symptoms of burnout include fatigue, anxiety, depression, and difficulty concentrating. It can also lead to physical health issues, such as headaches and muscle pain.

Anxiety is another common problem for entrepreneurs. Anxiety can manifest in different ways, such as feeling overwhelmed, being constantly vigilant, or having difficulty sleeping. It can also lead to physical health issues, such as headaches and digestive problems.

The good news is that there are steps that you can take as a founder to prioritise the well-being and stay healthy. The key is to maintain a balanced lifestyle. This means taking the time to rest and relax, setting limits and boundaries, and taking care of your physical and mental health.

While life will start to move really fast once your startup is up and running, just take a step back and make time for hobbies and interests outside of work. Pursuing hobbies and interests can be a great way to relax, recharge, and bring new ideas and perspectives back to the table.

Having a hobby or interest outside of work can be a great way to stay creative and inspired. Having something to look forward to outside of work can help you to stay productive and focused on the business goals. It can also help them better manage stress and keep a healthy work-life balance.

You must make time for activities that you enjoy and that help you to relax and recharge. This could be anything from reading, playing sports, or learning a new skill. It's important to make time for hobbies and interests that will allow you to step away from the work and get a different perspective.

Having a hobby or interest can also bring new ideas and perspectives back to the table. For example, a founder who loves to read may come across an article or book that can help them develop a new strategy for their business. Or, a founder who plays sports may come up with a creative way to solve a problem they're facing.

Maintaining a balanced lifestyle also leads to increased productivity:

If you are trying to work while being in a exhausted state, it's impossible to think clearly and do the work in hand properly. As a result, your productivity reduces greatly.

Maintaining a balanced lifestyle will have a positive impact on your productivity. It will allow you to improve your focus and give you the energy you need to be productive.

One of the most important aspects of a balanced lifestyle is getting enough sleep. When you are well-rested, you are more alert, this makes you able to think clearly. This can help you make better decisions and be more productive. Make sure that you are getting enough sleep, this can also help reduce stress and improve your overall health.

Another important aspect of a balanced lifestyle is eating right. Eating the right foods can give you the energy you need to stay productive. It can also help improve your focus and concentration. Eating a balanced diet full of fruits, vegetables, and lean proteins can help keep your energy levels up and your mind sharp.

Exercise is also a need for maintaining a balanced lifestyle. Exercise can help reduce stress, improve your mood, and increase your energy levels. It can also help you stay focused and alert, allowing you to be more productive.

Even while working for hours at a stretch, take breaks. Taking breaks throughout the day can help you stay focused and productive. Take a few minutes for yourself to stretch, take a walk, or grab a snack. This will help you stay refreshed and energised throughout the day.

Work-Life Balance:

It's no surprise that having a healthy work-life balance is essential for success. But how do you achieve this balance? One of the most important factors is setting boundaries between work and personal life.

Setting boundaries means setting realistic expectations for yourself and sticking to them. This could mean not checking emails after a certain hour, or scheduling certain days to be completely off the clock. By setting these boundaries, you're allowing yourself to take a break from work and focus on other aspects of your life.

Creating boundaries also helps you stay focused and be more productive during work hours. By having a set start and end time, you're creating a routine and structure that will help you stay on task. You're also more likely to be energised and engaged when you're working.

Setting boundaries is important for your mental health as well. When you're constantly connected to work, it can be hard to disconnect and relax. By setting boundaries, you're giving yourself the space to focus on other important aspects of your life.

It's important to remember that your startup is not your entire life, your family and friends too form an important part of life. Remember that you decided to start this journey to give a better life to your family, your absence doesn't give them the happy life you hoped for.

As a founder, it can be difficult to find the balance between work and personal life. Many entrepreneurs find themselves working long hours, feeling overwhelmed and exhausted, and neglecting the other important aspects of their life.

Having a healthy work-life balance can help you maintain better relationships with family and friends, and have a more fulfilling personal life. Make sure to schedule time for your family and friends, and make sure to stick to it. This will help you stay connected and build strong relationships, which can help you feel more fulfilled and balanced. Maintaining a balanced lifestyle is the ingredient to success, both in business and in life.

If you think that taking time for yourself to relax and recharge is laziness, it's not right, well by now we know know that it's absolutely not true. The truth is that taking care of yourself can be one of the best investments you can make in your business. When you're taking care of yourself, you're giving yourself the energy and focus you need to tackle the challenges that come with running a startup.

This final chapter serves as a reminder that taking care of yourself is not a luxury, but a necessity for achieving long-term success.

Thank you for joining us on this journey, and we wish you all the best in your startup endeavours.

ABOUT THE AUTHOR

Ex-Sgt Dasgupta is a man of many experiences and successes. Having served in the Indian Air Force for two decades, he gained invaluable knowledge and skills that helped him in his later years.

During his service, he was also entrusted with the responsibility of managing and running the messes of the military stations, which fuelled his interest in the food sector. It was during this time that he underwent several courses and specialist training in food production principles, fast food preparation, and various types of food preparation, where he was graded as exceptional in his trade proficiency. His dedication and commitment to his work earned him several commendations, and his skills as a steward, kitchen supervisor, and bakery manager were unparalleled.

After his retirement, Ex-Sgt Dasgupta continued to gain valuable experience while working as a production manager in a company. With his wife, Chandana J Dasgupta, and son's invaluable support, he started his very own bakery and restaurant business. Over the years, they slowly scaled their business into a full-fledged food production facility and a wholesale provider to a number of well-established bakeries across Vadodara, Gujarat.

Over a few years, the Dasgupta family scaled their business into a full-fledged food production facility and wholesale provider to a number of well-established bakeries across Vadodara, to further expand their revenue and business. They ran this business for close to two decades until their son successfully followed his passion to serve and fly in the services, after which Ex Sgt Dasgupta and his wife decided to retire. The business has led them to achieve financial freedom.

Ex-Sgt Dasgupta's journey has been one of resilience, perseverance, and hard work. He now shares his experience and knowledge with new-age entrepreneurs in the food industry through his book, "The Home Kitchen Startup". His aim is to show a clear path to those who aspire to build a great business for themselves and achieve financial freedom at an early age.

Kindly scan the above QR code to visit our page.

Please Don't Forget to provide your valuable review at
the store you purchased this book from.